THE JESSIE AND JOHN DANZ LECTURES

Facing the Threat of Nuclear Weapons

1989 Edition

Sidney D. Drell

With an Open Letter on the Danger of Thermonuclear War from Andrei Sakharov

UNIVERSITY OF WASHINGTON PRESS

Seattle and London

Library of Congress Cataloging in Publication Data

Drell, Sidney, 1926-
Facing the threat of nuclear weapons.

(The Jessie and John Danz lectures)
1. Atomic weapons and disarmament—Addresses, essays,
lectures. 2. Arms control—Addresses, essays, lectures.

I. Title. II. Series
JX 1974.7.D85 1983 327.1'74 83-6580
ISBN 0-295-96083-3

THE JESSIE AND JOHN DANZ LECTURES

In October 1961, Mr. John Danz, a Seattle pioneer, and his wife, Jessie Danz, made a substantial gift to the University of Washington to establish a perpetual fund to provide income to be used to bring to the University of Washington each year "distinguished scholars of national and international reputation who have concerned themselves with the impact of science and philosophy on man's perception of a rational universe." The fund established by Mr. and Mrs. Danz is now known as the Jessie and John Danz Fund, and the scholars brought to the University under its provisions are known as Jessie and John Danz Lecturers or Professors.

Mr. Danz wisely left to the Board of Regents of the University of Washington the identification of the special fields in science, philosophy, and other disciplines in which lectureships may be established. His major concern and interest were that the fund would enable the University of Washington to bring to the campus some of the truly great scholars and thinkers of the world.

Mr. Danz authorized the Regents to expend a portion of the income from the fund to purchase special collections of books, documents, and other scholarly materials needed to reinforce the effectiveness of the extraordinary lectureships and professorships. The terms of the gift also provided for the publication and dissemination, when this seems appropriate, of the lectures given by the Jessie and John Danz Lecturers.

Through this book, therefore, another Jessie and John Danz Lecturer speaks to the people and scholars of the world, as he has spoken to his audiences at the University of Washington and in the Pacific Northwest community.

Contents

Preface

In preparing my three Danz lectures, which with minor changes comprise this small volume, I set the following goal: to help the audience develop a better understanding of nuclear weapons and policy. I, therefore, began with a description of the physical realities of nuclear weapons and an analysis of the impact of these realities on policy and arms control negotiations. However, we all recognize that nuclear weapons present a fundamental moral, as well as physical, challenge. They are weapons of mass destruction on an unprecedented and unimaginable scale. Informed citizens and technical experts, together, share an obligation to help insure that a nuclear holocaust never occurs.

William Faulkner viewed the future pessimistically when he accepted the Nobel Prize for Literature in 1950: "Our tragedy today is a general and universal physical fear so long sustained by now that we can even bear it. There are no longer problems of the spirit. There is only the question: When will I be blown up?" With the recent creation of a large, active, and seemingly enduring public constituency in the Western World—a constituency that has thus far been politically effective and mostly constructive—I see grounds for a measure of optimism to replace Faulkner's pessimism. I hope this volume will in some measure add to the public understanding of nuclear weapons and policy and will thereby strengthen the grounds for my optimism.

I wish to thank the staff of the University of Washington Press for their excellent help in preparing the manuscript of my lectures for publication. With their cooperation I have updated the manuscript to take account of new developments during the month of May. I would like to thank Tanya Yankelevich, Andrei Sakharov's stepdaughter, her husband Efrem, and William Bundy, editor of *Foreign Affairs,* for permission to reprint Sakharov's open letter. Although I received Sakharov's letter after I delivered my Danz Lectures, he is speaking to many of the same issues that I address, and it seemed appropriate to include his letter in this volume.

May 31, 1983

Introduction to the 1989 Edition

The efforts of the United States and the Soviet Union to face the threat of nuclear weapons have passed through a turbulent period during the five years since these Danz Lectures were delivered at the University of Washington in the spring of 1983 and published in book form in the fall of that year.

The first two years were characterized by harsh rhetoric and little if any prospect of diplomatic progress. After the United States introduced ground-launched cruise missiles and extended-range Pershing II ballistic missiles in NATO at the end of 1983, formal negotiating efforts to limit deployment of strategic as well as intermediate-range offensive nuclear forces were suspended when the Soviet delegation walked out in Geneva. Instead, charges and countercharges of treaty violations were exchanged; efforts to resolve compliance issues broke down; some treaty provisions were abandoned (the SALT I and II numerical limits on strategic offensive forces by the United States), or violated (with continuing construction of the large-phased array radar by the Soviet Union at Krasnoyarsk in Siberia); and other treaty provisions were challenged by questionable actions. In the United States the debate over President Reagan's Strategic Defense Initiative (SDI or Star Wars) raged acrimoniously and intensely, and the administration sought a broad reinterpretation of the ABM Treaty of 1972 that would weaken it seriously, removing its restraints on developing and testing new technologies, the so-called "other physical principles." Even as it declared a unilateral moratorium on underground nuclear testing that lasted for sixteen months, the Soviet

Union pushed on with vigorous deployment of more SS-20 missiles targeted against Europe.

But in the next three years there occurred a radical turnaround with the resumption of a constructive dialogue and negotiation of a precedent-setting treaty removing intermediate-range nuclear forces. This INF Treaty removes totally and globally an entire category of weapons and introduces sweeping cooperative means of verification, including on-site inspection, that go far beyond what had been viewed as practical only a year earlier.

In time, historians will assign credit for this startling change: to General Secretary Mikhail Gorbachev, who ascended to the Soviet leadership in March 1985, two years after I gave these lectures, and with whom President Reagan has since met in four summits (more than have been attended by any other U.S. president since World War II); to new thinking by President Reagan and the ascendancy of the arms control and national security pragmatists in the last years of his administration; to the U.S. military buildup; to the Iran-Contra scandal; to economic realities; or to all of the above and more. Whatever the verdict of history, we can assess now the impact of recent events as the United States and the Soviet Union continue "facing the threat of nuclear weapons" during the coming decade. Although many details have changed, and the level of optimism therewith, fundamental issues raised in these lectures as originally delivered in 1983 are still with us.

The single most important concrete achievement since 1983 was the negotiation and ratification of the INF Treaty by the United States and the Soviet Union. It eliminates all ground-based missiles deployed and non-deployed of intermediate and shorter range, between 500 kilometers and 5,500 kilometers, along with the launchers, support structures, and support equipment. Numerically, this treaty is but a modest step. It removes less than 4 percent of the nuclear weapons in the world today, and it reduces NATO's deployed nuclear arsenal by roughly only 10 percent. But beyond these modest numerical achievements, the treaty is of historic importance for three reasons: first, its objective, the complete elimination of an entire class of U.S. and Soviet nuclear arms; second, the innovative character and scope of its verification provisions; and third, the achievement of a more stable situation via asymmetric reductions which, in this case, required the Soviet Union to remove almost four times as many deployed nuclear warheads and almost twice as many deployed missiles as the United States. The cooperative means of verification negotiated in the INF Treaty are an important supplement to the national technical means for verification of treaty compliance discussed in this book. They provide the groundwork for progress toward a firmer base for verifying future treaties; and they do so by finding that delicate balance which meets U.S. verification needs without exposing us to the danger of intelligence fishing expeditions by permitting "any-place-anytime" inspections that both sides would find unacceptable.

As to prospects for a treaty in the strategic arms reduction talks, or START, a broad framework has already been negotiated, based on a strong commitment by the two superpowers to make deep cuts in nuclear weapons deployed on systems of intercontinental range. The communique signed by President Reagan and General Secretary Gorbachev at the conclusion of the Washington summit in December 1987, and further confirmed in the Moscow summit of June 1988, is encouraging evidence that the United States and the Soviet Union are poised to move ahead from the INF Treaty to a much more important agreement reducing the number of these warheads by as much as a factor of two. The framework agreement calls for a limit of 1,600 launchers (ICBMs plus SLBMs plus strategic bombers); and of 4,900 ballistic missile warheads within a total of 6,000, including nuclear-armed weapons on bombers. The negotiators at START have also made considerable progress toward closure on a number of sublimits on individual weapons categories although several issues remain to be resolved in order to meet both countries' requirements for a stable balance. One notable provision is the agreement to cut in half the number of modern large ICBM's—i.e., the Soviet SS-18's—as well as the aggregate throw-weight of the Soviet ballistic missile force, below a ceiling applicable to both sides. However, the same issues that I described five years ago still present a major obstacle to completing a START treaty: survivable basing of the ICBM force; verification involving, in particular, new cruise missiles; and the future of the ABM Treaty and the Strategic Defense Initiative.

The MX missile still plays a central role in these considerations. In the aftermath of the Scowcroft Report the United States is deploying 50 MXs with 500 warheads in fixed silos, a decision that in no way addresses the problem of ICBM survivability that has been a central theme in discussions of strategic policy and planning for the past decade. Still at issue is what the United States should do to maintain a modern and survivable ICBM force. Should we deploy more highly MIRVed MX missiles, or deploy a larger number of mobile single-warhead ICBMs as recommended in the Scowcroft Report? How should these additional ICBMs be based?

Nuclear-armed long-range sea-launched cruise missiles present the most difficult of the current verification challenges. In the summit communique both countries committed themselves to negotiate ceilings on the deployment of such missiles and to seek mutually acceptable and effective methods of verification of such limitations, but these have not yet been worked out. The problem is that SLCMs are small and easy to hide; they do not require fancy launchers; they can be widely deployed on many ships; and they can play a dual role with conventional or nuclear warheads.

The final issue that still remains central to the negotiations is the future of the ABM Treaty, and what effort in research and development in anti-ballistic missile technology can and should be pursued. In particular how does the treaty apply to the new technologies, the "other physical principles"? Are they restricted when it comes to testing and development, as specified in the 1972 treaty, or do they escape those restrictions as advocated in the broad interpretation of the treaty propounded by the administration in 1985? The issue, although not fully resolved in the U.S. domestic debate, has led to congressional legislation limiting Star Wars spending to those activities consistent with the treaty as traditionally interpreted. In the spring of 1988 the Defense Science Board's report on the SDI to Secretary of Defense Frank Carlucci also recommended that work in the initial phase remain consistent with the traditional interpretation.

Ever the optimist, I believe that the U.S.-Soviet arms control negotiations so far have provided the basis for sensible compromise that may still make a START treaty a reality during 1989. The United States should meet its requirements for a survivable ICBM force by deploying single-warhead missiles within launcher and warhead limits as already agreed to at START. Initially these ICBMs should be deployed in fixed hardened silos. The rationale for this basing is that single-warhead missiles are not valuable enough to be worthy of attack in an arms control framework that limits warheads equally on both sides. The attacker would be required to expend more warheads than he could destroy. However, as a hedge against future needs, should START fail, the missile should be designed to be capable of being transferred to a mobile deployment that would be highly survivable but also considerably more expensive.

I support a compromise on U.S.-Soviet differences on strategic defense research and on the cruise missile problem. It would be simple and mutually beneficial to agree that all work on strategic defense in the United States and the Soviet Union during the coming decade should be consistent with the traditional interpretation of the ABM Treaty. It is my technical judgment that such a requirement to comply with the ABM Treaty will pose no harmful technological burden on a properly constructed U.S. program. The research work carried out under the SDI program since President Reagan's speech in 1983 has taught much about the new technologies, but no lesson is more significant and persuasive than our awareness of the enormous gap between where we are now and what will be needed for an effective defense. As was true in 1983, we do not know how to bridge it. Likewise, it would be in our mutual interest to recognize that accurately verifiable numerical restraints on long-range sea-launched cruise missiles with nuclear warheads are not crucial owing to their limited targeting potential. Therefore, in the words of Ambassador Max Kampelman, for both problems we should "kick the can down the road" and sign a START treaty, supplemented by mutual commitments for the coming decade that (1) neither side will deploy more than a small number (300 to 500) of nuclear-armed long-range SLCMs and (2) both sides will remain true to the traditionally interpreted ABM Treaty.

Many additional issues addressed in the 1983 lectures remain. Battlefield nuclear weapons still cast a long shadow by their ominous presence. Although chemical weapons limitations or bans have yet to be negotiated, talks have progressed in a spirit of cooperation and more openness about cooperative verification. In addition, the Soviet Union has responded to requests for details about the anthrax-caused deaths of Sverdlovsk, in accord with the 1972 Biological Weapons Convention.

Talks are continuing on ratification of the Threshold Test Ban Treaty (TTBT). There is now broad recognition that the 150-kiloton ceiling for underground nuclear tests has been adhered to satisfactorily and that further reductions of the threshold to a few kilotons can be monitored and verified by unmanned seismic stations. But the talks have not come to fruition. The talks on mutual and balanced force reductions on conventional military forces in Europe have accomplished little. They are now to be succeeded by a new venue for NATO–Warsaw Pact mandate talks toward achieving what General Secretary Gorbachev has called "defensive sufficiency." This will require a major force restructuring as well as reductions in order to remove the threat of "blitzkrieg" present in the current confrontation of massed armor and artillery.

Significant progress in crisis prevention and risk reduction has been made with the agreement between the United States and the Soviet Union to create national risk-reduction centers and to improve "hot line" communications. In addition, the thirty-five-nation European Disarmament Conference completed an agreement in 1986 on confidence-building measures in Europe, including provisions for prior notification of military exercises with lead times of as long as two years in some cases, and for mutually observing such maneuvers. In fact, this agreement set the important precedent of permitting on-site inspection in the Soviet Union.

Overall, one sees in this pattern of activity a measure of progress and increased reason for hope that the U.S. and Soviet governments are currently embarked on a path of constructive and cautious cooperation, not only toward achieving further progress in arms control but also toward improving our overall political dialogue and resolving regional crises that might trigger superpower conflict.

As a final note, I take special pleasure in being able to report that at the end of 1986 Andrei Sakharov and Yelena Bonner were released from internal exile in Gorky and have returned to Moscow. Andrei has returned to a more normal life, as a physicist as well as an outspoken advocate of recent Soviet reforms, including in particular more openness (*glasnost*) and improved human rights.

August 25, 1988

FACING THE THREAT OF
NUCLEAR WEAPONS

Challenge to Survival

In the long battle for survival of the species, aggression and combat have been central factors. The assertion and the defense of one's rights and essential needs have regulated relations between individuals, families, and tribes of different species all the way up the evolutionary ladder. Konrad Lorenz, in his engaging book *King Solomon's Ring,* describes how different species have flourished or withered depending on their ability to limit and terminate their struggles among themselves to enforce their territorial imperative.

The human species asserts its position at the top of the evolutionary ladder and assumes its special mission not only to endure but, indeed, to prevail at that lofty pinnacle. But we also face a very special peril.

The extraordinary achievements of the human spirit and genius on which we base our claims to preeminence have also handed us our gravest threat. Out of our understanding of Nature we have created the nuclear means to destroy our civilization, if not our very own existence.

Can we avoid the fate of a nuclear holocaust? We can never undo or unlearn the knowledge of nuclear explosions—of fission and fusion. Our challenge is to develop new means for regulating our differences and settling our conflicts. War is no longer acceptable, for as President Eisenhower cautioned back in 1956 at the dawn of the thermonuclear age, war has become "destruction of the enemy and suicide." Albert Einstein remarked shortly after the first atom bomb was exploded that we have to change our ways of thinking, warning: "The unleashed power of the atom has changed everything save our modes of thinking; we thus drift toward an unparalleled catastrophe." More recently, Pope John Paul II emphasized the moral dimension of the challenge, when in the poignant setting of the memorial to the dead at Hiroshima in 1981, he expressed this appeal: "Our future on this planet, exposed as it is to nuclear annihilation, depends on one single factor. Humanity must make a moral about-face."

The avoidance of a nuclear holocaust is the absolute moral and political imperative of our time. It is our greatest challenge. Will we succeed? Because, at heart, I am an optimist, I believe we will. But it is not from human history that I derive my optimism. We know that, over the full span of human records, there have been wars, and furthermore that human beings have used every means available to kill and overpower one another. I was reminded by my Stanford colleague, philosopher Philip Rhinelander, that Pope Innocent II, in the year 1139, declared the recently developed crossbow "hateful to God and unfit for Christians" and forbade its use.* Historians record, however, that this

---

*See Philip H. Rhinelander, "Peace: The Ultimate Challenge," *The Stanford Magazine* (Winter 1982).

edict of the Second Lateran Council was amended to permit use of the crossbow against the Moslems, and that this limitation also soon broke down as Christians took up the crossbow against one another before it was superseded by more efficient means of killing. What rational basis is there, then, for optimism? My optimism is sustained by one slender fact and one article of faith.

The fact is this: almost thirty-eight years have passed since the first atom bombs devastated Hiroshima and Nagasaki, and during all that time our fear, revulsion, and respect for nuclear weapons have been compelling in restraining us from using them—in spite of the numerous conflicts and opportunities to do so.

The article of faith is, simply, that we *will* succeed in preventing the searing memories of Hiroshima from fading away. The recent resurgence of public interest and concern about the danger of nuclear weapons and holocaust helps sustain this faith. So does the evidence that growing segments of the public recognize that the possibility and even the threat of ever using nuclear weapons of mass destruction against innocent people poses a major moral as well as technical and physical dilemma for society. As a society, we are, if anything, growing increasingly sensitive to the fact that nuclear weapons are fundamentally different because of the enormity of their destructive power—including their deadly dangerous and long-lived radioactive memory. Perhaps we have now achieved what Alfred Nobel, the inventor of dynamite, hoped for when he said: "I wish I could produce a substance or a machine of such frightful efficacy for wholesale devastation that wars should thereafter become altogether impossible."*

In this chapter I will describe the nuclear realities and the nuclear difference and discuss deterrence—in concept and in practice. In my second chapter I will discuss nuclear arms control, exploring in some depth verification requirements and different paths to progress. My final chapter is concerned with a more personal topic, the dilemma faced by all scientists—and highlighted in the ordeals of Robert Oppenheimer and Andrei Sakharov—when they have become involved in issues of public policy of which nuclear weapons are an especially important example. In that chapter I include a discussion of the significance and implications of the President's call, in a March 1983 speech, for a space-age star wars defense.

EFFECTS OF NUCLEAR WAR

Nuclear bombs are not just one more weapon. You have heard frequently, but let me recall very briefly, the huge scale of their destructive effects. Nuclear bombs exceed the largest bombs of the prenuclear era by factors as large as a million. Their destructive energy release—or so-called yield—is measured in megatons (millions of tons of TNT equivalent). The sum total of munitions expended in World War II from 1939 to 1945 added up to less than 6 megatons. That is less than the megatonnage of *one* of the large nuclear warheads now deployed. Hiroshima and Naga-saki were devastated by "relatively small" bombs

*Quoted in Rhinelander, "Peace: The Ultimate Challenge."

whose yields were little more than one-hundredth of a megaton.

No one within 10 miles of a one-megaton bomb is likely to emerge unscathed.

Radioactive fallout is the unique signature of a nuclear explosion. Its lethal effect is greatly increased if the explosion is near enough to the ground to vaporize thousands of tons of earth in the hot nuclear fireball. The soil mixed together with radioactive debris from the bomb subsequently rises to the stratosphere as the characteristic mushroom cloud. The heavier particles start settling within hours as fine, deadly radioactive ash. For each one megaton detonated this ash, driven by the wind, will typically make 1,000 square miles of the earth's surface uninhabitable to unsheltered humans for several or more weeks. The lighter particles rise into the stratosphere, circulating around the world for months and even years before returning to the ground as worldwide fallout.

By any measure, nuclear weapons are weapons of mass destruction. The explosion of just one medium-size bomb over Seattle—or any metropolitan area of comparable size—would cause one of history's greatest disasters, killing and injuring close to a million people.

There are no disputes about the physical facts of a nuclear explosion as I have described them. Where the problems arise is when one tries to understand what has led the United States and the Soviet Union to arm ourselves to the point that today our arsenals bulge with more than 50,000 nuclear weapons with the total explosive power of some one million Hiroshimas.

What in the world can a sane people do with such vast quantities of destructive power? Official estimates are that a combined total of more than 200 million American and Soviet citizens would be killed outright in a major nuclear exchange which was designed to kill civilians. The "initial" survivors, a very large number of whom would be seriously injured, would face the longer-term, more subtle, but nonetheless hideous effects of radioactive fallout and infectious diseases (such as cholera and dysentery) due to poor sanitation; and this is a prospect they would face without anything like adequate medical support. As emphasized by all responsible studies in and out of government, the catastrophe of a major nuclear war is so far beyond human experience and imagination that the dreadful unknowns dwarf the calculable and predictable effects.

In a 1976 pamphlet, the U.S. Arms Control and Disarmament Agency (ACDA) emphasized that much of our knowledge of the effects of nuclear explosions was gained by chance and that this "should imbue us with humility as we contemplate the remaining uncertainties (as well as the certainties) about nuclear warfare." At that time, Dr. Fred Iklé, currently undersecretary for defense for policy, was director of ACDA. In the foreword he wrote to this pamphlet he observed: "Uncertainty is one of the major conclusions in our studies, as the haphazard and unpredicted derivation of many of our discoveries emphasizes. Moreover, it now appears that a massive attack with many large-scale nuclear detonations could cause such widespread and long-lasting environmental damage that the aggressor country might suffer serious physiological, economic, and environmental effects even without a nuclear response by the country attacked."*

With the passage of time, uncertainty about the global consequences of a major nuclear war has endured. For instance, there very well could be widespread, long-lasting, and potentially catastrophic environmental damage due to depletion of ozone in the stratosphere which shields us from the sun's ultraviolet radiation. The resulting adverse consequences include increased incidence of skin cancer in fair-skinned races and decreased crop yields.

Another possible result of a major nuclear war is the igniting of tremendous fires in vast forest, cropland, and urban and industrial areas. The fires could persist for months and completely disrupt agricultural production in the northern hemisphere if they occurred during the growing season. From this follow other consequences of social and economic disruption, not to mention the psychological strain of such a massive trauma to all the survivors.

THE MORAL ISSUE

The unprecedented scale of destruction and devastation of which nuclear weapons are capable presents us with fundamental issues—moral as well as practical.

As a scientist, it is natural for me to approach the issues of war and peace with a technical orientation. That is my strength and experience as I work to understand the physical realities of nuclear weapons and I

Worldwide Effects of Nuclear War—Some Perspectives (U.S. Arms Control and Disarmament Agency, 1976).

study how these physical realities impose limitations on the available alternatives for national policy. These are important issues. But I am also a human being and I understand that the challenge of nuclear weapons is ultimately a moral challenge, for these are weapons of mass destruction. This moral dimension of the challenge was instantly recognized by scientists acquainted with the vast and indiscriminate destruction they could cause, and was summarized very powerfully by the great physicists Enrico Fermi and I. I. Rabi in their personal addendum to the 1949 report of the General Advisory Committee of the Atomic Energy Commission on the decision whether or not to develop the first thermonuclear weapon, the "super":

> It is clear that the use of such a weapon cannot be justified on any ethical ground which gives a human being a certain individuality and dignity even if he happens to be a resident of an enemy country.
>
> The fact that no limits exist to the destructiveness of this weapon makes its very existence and the knowledge of its construction a danger to humanity as a whole. It is necessarily an evil thing considered in any light.*

Today—just one-third of a century after Fermi and Rabi wrote those words at the dawn of the thermonuclear era—we recognize that the vast arsenals of these weapons of mass destruction that we have already accumulated could shatter the civilization created by

* Quoted in Herbert York, *The Advisors: Oppenheimer, Teller, and the Superbomb* (San Francisco: W. H. Freeman, 1975).

human genius and inspiration over our entire recorded history of some thirty centuries. What right has man to cause—or even threaten—such a devastating insult to the earth, the ecosphere, the very condition of human existence? If modern civilization is to improve its chances for avoiding nuclear holocaust in the long run, I believe it is absolutely necessary to return the nuclear debate to such fundamental issues.

Deterrence

In addition to the moral issue, we face a practical issue as a result of the enormity of the devastating potential of nuclear weapons. Simply, it is a fact that any nation initiating a nuclear war may be literally committing suicide. This fact is based on a technical reality that is almost universally recognized: there is no effective defense against nuclear retaliation. There is no technology known today, or on the technological horizon reaching into the future to the end of this century, that is capable of repelling an attack against our nation by thousands of nuclear warheads in their intercontinental missile paths that span distances of 6,000 miles in less than a thirty-minute flight time.

This physical reality was recognized in 1972 when we and the Soviet Union agreed to sign the SALT I treaty that severely limits the deployment of antiballistic missile defenses—or ABM systems. That treaty is of unlimited duration and is in force today. During the past decade since that treaty went into effect, there have been technical advances: advances in radar, missile, and computer technologies for both the offensive and defensive systems. However, on technical grounds

I still see no prospect whatsoever of deploying—on the ground or in space, with missiles or lasers—an effective defense of the nation's people and cities. I shall return to this question in my third chapter. President Reagan gave it prominence in his speech of March 23, 1983, by calling for a defensive umbrella over the United States against nuclear attack. The President's plans and his goals notwithstanding, there remains a physical reality of nature: owing to the very great destructive power of nuclear weapons, the offense has—and can maintain—a predominance over the defense. The situation differs greatly from World War II when the Royal Air Force won the Battle of Britain by destroying one in ten German planes per attack. The German air force could not endure such losses, and, even though nine out of ten planes got through the defenses, London survived its extinguishable fires. Contrast this with the nuclear era today. No matter how effective the defense, if it is less than perfect it fails, for it takes but one medium-size bomb on target to extinguish Seattle. If only one out of twenty—or 5 percent—of the Soviet missiles were to arrive at American cities, our *immediate* casualties would very likely number in the many tens of millions, or more, and our industry and our major cities would be reduced to radioactive rubble.

I also cannot conceive of a civil defense system that could protect our society—or the Soviet society—from the unprecedented disaster and devastation of a nuclear war. It is understandable that civil defense has entered prominently into our national security debates for more than twenty years, because it touches the basic human instinct of survival. The potential for disaster is ever present in our society, and it hardly seems prudent to make no plans for survival or recovery in the event of a natural or man-made disaster or accident, nuclear or otherwise. But it would be a very misleading and dangerous illusion to view civil defense as substantially increasing the likelihood of survival or of recovery in a major nuclear war.

The basic technical realities of nuclear weapons as I have described them present a stark picture for us all to recognize. Defenseless against these nuclear weapons of mass destruction, we live in a balance of terror as mutual hostages in today's world. This is a situation unprecedented in history. In the past, tribes, nations, and alliances have organized to protect their vital interests—their people, their cities and industry, their trade. They have done this by preparing to destroy an opponent's military forces in combat. This is no longer possible. As President Eisenhower said back in 1956: "We're rapidly getting to the point that no war can be won." It is no longer battle to exhaustion and surrender; the outlook now comes close to "destruction of the enemy *and* suicide." There will, indeed, be no winners in a nuclear war. I conclude, therefore, that the sole purpose of nuclear weapons is, and must remain for as long as they are deployed, to deter nuclear war.

Deterrence is the key concept of the nuclear age. It requires of us a new common sense. Although it has stood the test of time for the more than two decades since both powers have had the ability to destroy each other, it is under siege from a chorus of critics with many voices. A clear understanding of what deterrence means must underpin any discussion or explanation of nuclear policy and weapons. Deterrence has three essential ingredients: one is a state of mind expressing a national will. A second is the military capability to retaliate with assured destruction. A policy of deterrence must make clear to anyone who contemplates starting a nuclear war against the United States and its allies that he would be putting his own society—his people, his cities, and his industry—at risk to an intolerable level of devastation. Rational behavior by governments and their leaders is the third essential ingredient of deterrence. Once they recognize the risks of starting a nuclear war they must act accordingly and thus be deterred. Except for the fact that it has worked for the past two decades, there isn't very much that is attractive about nuclear deterrence. It is of questionable morality, of unquestioned danger, and—as a child of the nuclear revolution—devoid of historical pedigree. Despite these blemishes it is the only game in town, and this fact has to be understood.

Some critics challenge deterrence as immoral for threatening tens and hundreds of millions of helpless citizens with annihilation, and they criticize it as based on a logical paradox for making threats that would be suicidal to implement. Such criticism is pretty strong and on target. Nevertheless, unless—or until—the human species makes that next great evolutionary advance by learning to resolve our differences peacefully and, as a result, removes the scourge of weapons and war from the face of this planet, I see—on technical grounds alone—no escape from the mutual hostage relationship and no choice but to make deterrence work. This is our immediate task and, to use an old Navy phrase, "to get by on *our* watch" in the decade ahead.

The Pastoral Letter on "The Challenge of Peace" which was adopted on May 3, 1983, by the National

Conference of Catholic Bishops on War and Peace is a remarkable document—powerful as well as important—that probes the moral dilemma of deterrence. It asks important questions; it analyzes them skillfully; it is written clearly; and, I would add, it comes to the correct conclusions. After grappling with the basic issue of the immorality of threatening massive slaughter of the innocents, it arrives at the judgment that "deterrence cannot be accepted as 'an end in itself' " but continues that, since it offers the best promise of avoiding nuclear war, "deterrence may still be judged as morally acceptable provided it is used as a step toward progressive disarmament." To me this is precisely the new common sense of nuclear weapons expressed simply and clearly.* There is no Pentagonese in these words.

Other critics challenge deterrence as a policy that violates the old common sense—the traditional wisdom— that nations must have military forces capable of attacking and destroying an aggressor's military strength, thereby reducing the damage they themselves will suffer if attacked. In today's jargon this military capability is known as "counterforce." This requirement for counterforce is above and beyond what is often referred to as "flexible response." Flexible response means the ability to respond in measure with

---

*The words quoted above are taken from the Second Draft of the Pastoral Letter. The Third (and final) Draft, as adopted overwhelmingly by the bishops' conference, quotes Pope John Paul II's judgment that "deterrence may still be judged morally acceptable, 'certainly not as an end in itself but as a step on the way toward progressive disarmament.' " The Draft adds further: "Progress toward a world free of dependence on deterrence must be carefully carried out. But it must not be delayed."

the provocation and is a reality of today's nuclear forces; they can be launched selectively or massively against an extensive repertoire of targets. But counterforce weapons, if deployed in large numbers, directly threaten to destroy significant parts of an opponent's retaliatory forces. This threat to his deterrent raises a major problem. On one hand, it is infeasible, on technical grounds alone, to disarm an opponent. On the other hand, as each country faces a growing counterforce threat to its retaliatory forces it will simply build more—and we'll witness an open-ended arms race. A clear choice must be made: either to follow the old way of thinking with counterforce or to go with the existing physical facts of deterrence. There is a clear distinction between these two policies, and we cannot have it both ways!

The United States and the Soviet Union have the choice: either to focus on expanding threats to one another's retaliatory forces or to give emphasis to maintaining the security of these forces. This issue of counterforce versus deterrence is becoming increasingly important to resolve because the technology of delivering nuclear weapons has continued to advance with impressive virtuosity. In particular, the accuracy and the reliability of the missile delivery systems have turned them into very effective means for attacking an opponent's land-based missiles housed in hardened underground silos that were heretofore viewed as invulnerable and safe. Furthermore, the fact that a single missile can deliver a large number of nuclear warheads with precision to a wide range of individual targets via the technology of MIRVs (multiple independently targetable reentry vehicles) makes them economically attractive and practical to proliferate. And, indeed, their number is growing rapidly.

Advocates of counterforce have recently been advertising their policy as meriting a seal of superior morality by emphasizing that it targets limited or controlled strikes against military and counterforce targets as opposed to an attack in full force against cities and hundreds of millions of people. Given the nuclear realities, how realistic, in fact, are such speculations and planning for "limited" nuclear war-fighting and counterforce attacks? How would, or could, the conflict be managed—and terminated—without escalation to all-out destruction?

Neither past experience nor war-gaming gives cause for much hope that the nuclear exchange and resulting devastation would remain limited and aimed exclusively at military targets. There is a great danger that, once the vital interests of the United States and the Soviet Union are engaged to the point that either initiates a nuclear attack, both countries will dig ever deeper into their vast arsenals of more than 50,000 nuclear weapons. In addition, there is no *technical* basis for any confidence that it will be possible to control the escalation of a limited nuclear conflict. Once the nuclear threshold is crossed, there will inevitably be a broad delegation of authority down the line for nuclear release. This is required by the very short missile flight times and by the potential vulnerabilities of any conceivable worldwide command, control, and communication system from a national command center to the broadly dispersed military units with thousands of nuclear weapons.

We are all familiar with the theoreticians and strategists heavily armed with computer printouts describing scenarios of limited nuclear conflicts with low casualties followed by rapid recovery. Given the lack of relevant data for input, it is amazing how many analyses of this kind one sees and how greatly exaggerated are the claims that are based on them.

Our extensive history of real wars—the nonnuclear conflicts of the past—has taught us to appreciate how vitally sensitive the course of events is to factors such as surprise, determination, luck, and individual acts of bravery and leadership. Perhaps that is why there are so few detailed calculations and claims for such conflicts. The data available from real wars—the nonnuclear conflicts we know only too well—have generated a healthy measure of humility, and call to mind the remark by Dame Rebecca West: "Before a war, military science seems like a real science, like astronomy; but after a war, it seems more like astrology."

When you hear claims made by individuals on the basis of their studies and calculations—but almost no data—as to how much civil defense will contribute to our survival, and thereby to an ultimate victory in a nuclear war, keep in mind how rapidly individual units of society descend to chaos and fall apart at much lower levels of stress: remember what happens during sudden blackouts. It makes you wonder how societies will react after just one thermonuclear weapon has hit, much less a hundred or several thousand. The fascination with such calculations reminds me of the exchange in act 1 of George Bernard Shaw's *Major Barbara* between Lomax, a young man-about-town, and Andrew Undershaft, a millionaire munitions manufacturer. To Lomax's comment: "Well, the more destructive war becomes, the sooner it will be abolished, eh?" Undershaft retorts: "Not at all. The more destructive war becomes, the more fascinating we find it."

On this score of limited nuclear war, I more highly value the experience and wisdom of General David C. Jones, former chairman of the Joint Chiefs of Staff, who said very simply and to the point at the time of his retirement in June of 1982: "I don't see much chance of a nuclear war being limited or protracted."

DETERRENCE AND THE MX

The seemingly endless debate over the MX missile illustrates and emphasizes my concern that today there is still a lot of confusion about the meaning of deterrence and the purpose of our nuclear forces. This confusion was already evident back in the early 1970s when the United States first made the fateful decision—an awful decision for our own self-interest—to develop and deploy the MIRVs that turned each of our missiles into a hydra-headed monster with many bombs aimed very precisely at different targets. Our original justification for MIRVs was that they would penetrate ballistic missile defenses by overwhelming their defensive firepower with an intense rain of many warheads. They were offered as an insurance policy against possible, if yet unrealized, Soviet ABM deployments. When, however, the SALT I treaty of 1972 prohibited the deployment of nationwide ABM defenses, U.S. MIRV programs proceeded full tilt. The new rationale for MIRVs became our alleged need for counterforce—the need to threaten Soviet retaliatory forces. As stated (in a speech to the U.S. Air Force As-

19

sociation) in late 1970 by General John D. Ryan, then chief of staff of the U.S. Air Force, the MIRVed Minuteman III missile "will be our best means of destroying the time-urgent targets like the long range weapons of the enemy."

Thinking back to those times, as one heavily involved as a member of the President's Science Advisory Committee, I recall how little attention the MIRV issue received from the media and the public during the crucial years of decision with so much attention riveted on Vietnam and subsequently on Watergate. Deterrence and arms control both lost that round. Predictably, Soviet MIRV deployments followed those of the United States four years later and have continued up to the present with considerable intensity in their SS-18 and SS-19 programs.

There is a sense of *déjà vu* in today's debate over the MX. Do we want simple deterrence based on survivable forces or do we want counterforce? This debate is being covered much more thoroughly than the original MIRV decision, and I think very effectively in our regional as well as the national press, TV, and radio. Recall that the original rationale for developing the MX was to decrease the vulnerability of our land-based missile force and improve deterrence. We sought to base the new ICBM so that it could not be attacked and destroyed. Now four years later and after some thirty-four or so different basing schemes have been considered—I've lost the precise count—from dirigibles and Bigbirds to sandhogs, dragstrips, and Densepacks, what do we hear today as the rationale for MX? The theme has changed from deterrence to counterforce, to judge by many statements by both civilian and military officials. Thus Air Force Major General James McCarthy testified to Congress late in 1982 that with the MX "we put hard targets (such as Soviet missile silos) at risk, which is the principal reason why we need the MX missile." Congress temporarily shelved the MX because it was not persuaded—and correctly so—that any of the proposed schemes were effective for deterrence or worth the cost. Claims of the survivability and effectiveness of Densepack, Bigbird, and Racetrack—the three schemes with, at one time or another, administration backing—just don't stand up under close technical scrutiny. What is still not clear in our MX debate is whether the United States will opt for improving deterrence by improving the ability of our overall retaliatory strength to survive any attack targeted against it or whether we will insist on trumping the Soviets at a higher and more dangerous level of counterforce.

The President's Commission on Strategic Forces, chaired by Lieutenant General Brent Scowcroft (ret.), former National Security advisor to President Ford, has now completed its work.* Its report on modernization of the strategic forces of the United States, and the President's decisions, has triggered a much-needed national debate: What do we really mean by deterrence? What forces do we require to maintain a stable deterrence through the 1990s? How should we manage our force modernization to help achieve our arms control goals, considered as a prime factor and not merely an add-on to our weapons decisions?

*See Appendix for a comment on the Scowcroft Report and the MX.

This debate will offer a major opportunity and challenge to the nation—the leaders, the citizens, and the media—which can and hopefully will provide the appropriate context and ask the right questions, with common sense and clarity. It is a sorely needed debate, because it provides an opportunity to clarify the present confusion as to where we are and what's happening in this area of nuclear armaments and policy.

This confusion has been acute since 1980, when many people were shocked to hear our leaders allege for the first time that the American nuclear deterrent was no longer secure and that America was behind the USSR. A major program was initiated to modernize our nuclear forces in order to catch up with the Soviet Union and close a dangerous "window of vulnerability." Is it true that our deterrent really is inadequate? What more do we require?

U.S. and Soviet forces are very different, having developed out of different technological and bureaucratic styles and geographic needs. In particular, the Soviets emphasized the strength of their land-based force of large ICBMs, while America wisely focused its best technology on the mobile and quiet, and therefore untargetable, submarine-based systems and on long-range strategic bombers that can take off and fly out on warning of attack.

But both countries have deployed far more forces than are required for deterrence. The Soviets have an edge in total megatonnage on their intercontinental systems, while the U.S. edge is in numbers of warheads on strategic systems. The total Soviet force is estimated to be about 5,000 megatons compared to a U.S. total of 3,000. The Soviet Union currently has more than 7,000 nuclear warheads on its intercontinental systems, the bulk of which are deployed on their land-based ICBMs. The United States has more than 9,000 nuclear warheads on its intercontinental-range strategic systems, and the vast majority of these are deployed securely and effectively for retaliatory purposes, no matter what the level of enemy action. What more is required for deterrence? When one starts counting and comparing numbers, it is easy to forget that a very small fraction of these nuclear bombs would cause greater damage than mankind has ever conceived of. That fact—and not small numerical differences—is the important message. Given that fact and the overall security of our deterrent strength, how can one understand Defense Secretary Weinberger's statement to a group of Harvard students in the summer of 1982: "I worry that we will not have enough time to get strong enough to prevent nuclear war."

It is one thing to call, quite sensibly, for the improvement of the strategic deterrent by further strengthening its ability to survive direct attack. But such a grossly exaggerated statement, quite at odds with reality, causes alarm and confusion about U.S. nuclear policy. And rightly so! We are not behind the Russians. Windows of vulnerability appear only to those who disregard the overall balance of forces and myopically insist on very selective measures of force comparison. You can make the United States look as if it's ahead by counting total numbers of warheads or the Soviets even more so by counting only ICBM warheads and megatonnage.

One has to watch out for—and aggressively challenge—conclusions from very biased comparisons, as well as the fundamental assumptions underlying them. I can assure you that physicists are well aware of how badly we can be misled in our laboratories on the basis of selected and biased data samples. In search of nuclear understanding it is so important to ask the questions and raise the issues that matter and to avoid largely irrelevant, if simplistic, "bean counting" comparisons.

WHO'S AHEAD?

I think it is time—and the need has never been more urgent—for us to return to the basics and to common sense in facing the nuclear challenge. We have to stop being prisoners of numbers and "who's ahead?" thinking. At today's levels of nuclear weapons, the question of "who's ahead?" has lost meaning. We have to keep in mind what these weapons do. We have to realize that nuclear weapons are so destructive and their danger is so great that we cannot buy security by greater nuclear strength. Quite the contrary! With growing nuclear arsenals—and particularly with growing numbers of nuclear armed nations—it is our insecurity that is increasing. We need not the MX but effective arms control to improve our national security.

With regard to our vast nuclear armories that are continually being refined and polished and admired, I am reminded of the famous lines from Alexander Pope's "Essay on Man":

> Vice is a monster of so frightful mien,
> As to be hated, needs but to be seen;
> Yet seen too oft, familiar with her face,
> We first endure, then pity, then embrace.

Recall how Pope continues:

> But where th' Exteme of Vice, was ne'er agreed.

and concludes:

> No creature owns it in the first degree,
> But thinks his neighbor further gone than he;

In a nutshell that expresses our dilemma. Consumed by a detailed, quantitative balancing of the nuclear vice that we have learned to endure and now embrace, each country accuses the other of owning more of what is evil than it possesses, and our nuclear debates and discussions have become like those of scholastics of the thirteenth century to whom the fundamental ethical and moral issues of religion had degenerated largely to questions of how many angels can fit on the head of a pin. I can draw the macabre parallel of how for us the nuclear debate has similarly been reduced to how many MIRVs fit on the head of our modern pins, the ICBMs.* And just as the desolation and devastation of the fourteenth century, with the hundred years of wars, followed the thirteenth century, are we destined to a similar or a worse fate in the twenty-first century? Will future historians, if there are any, look back on the second half of the twentieth century as the golden age of nuclear scholastics?

If modern civilization is to improve its chances for avoiding nuclear holocaust in the long run, it is abso-

---

*See the preface to *Endgame: The Inside Story of Salt II* by Strobe Talbott (New York: Harper and Row, 1979).

lutely necessary to return to fundamental issues. As a start, both the United States and the Soviet Union must break the "monkey-see, monkey-do" pattern that has guided us in the past as we have pushed on to new technologies and growing numbers of nuclear bombs. In its place we need to focus more on the technical realities of nuclear weapons. Both the United States and the Soviet Union must base their security policy and their nuclear weapons decisions simply and clearly on the criterion of maintaining a secure and reliable deterrent and not any further requirements of counterforce or limited nuclear war-fighting that are generally as limitless as they are unrealistic. And we must pursue arms control negotiations vigorously and in good faith toward strengthening deterrence at lower levels of confidently survivable retaliatory forces.

Toward a Public Constituency for Arms Control

I have one last observation in this chapter. It has often been said that war is too important to be left to the generals and that peace is too vital to be left to the politicians. So are matters of nuclear weapons and policy too important to be left to the experts. Nuclear weapons and policies are matters of life and death, for our entire planet; and life and death are matters of importance to us all. All of us are the targets of these undiscriminating weapons of mass destruction. There is, therefore, no excuse for us not to constitute an *informed and an effective public constituency* insisting on the imperative of arms control.

I am greatly encouraged by the recent resurgence of public interest in and concern about the nuclear weapons danger—at both the technical and the moral levels. The public arms control constituency created during the past year must continue to grow and prove that it is enduring, informed, constructive, and energetic and has a broad political base. That will require a continued effort by all of us. I credit the freeze movement with playing a vital role in creating this constituency, which was lacking for more than twenty years—and was sorely missed at the time of the Senate's failure to ratify the SALT II treaty.

I wish to be clear that as a technician I find difficulties with a comprehensive freeze as literal policy. I also reject the suggestion that a freeze offers a realistic escape from serious, detailed negotiations. I have, however, supported the freeze campaign and I continue to support it as a mandate for arms control. I reject the claim by some of our leaders that the freeze movement weakens the U.S. position at the arms control negotiations by showing us as a divided country. Not so. Our strength as a democracy rests on the involvement and constructive efforts of an informed citizenry. I also reject the claim that there is a window of vulnerability that we must close by building more weapons before we can negotiate reductions. To me the primary importance of the freeze is that it has served as the first step in building a constituency by uniting many who found cause to reject both the record of the past and the rhetoric of the present in arms control. And with good cause. The record of past arms control negotiations carried on without mutual restraint in weapons programs has seen the number of strategic nuclear warheads triple after thirteen years of negotiation. The rhetoric of the present is to emphasize counterforce and limited nuclear war-fighting at the expense of deterrence.

It is a welcome and important development that the citizenry has finally concluded that in this vital issue of life and death it is unacceptable to abdicate responsibility to the experts alone. We all have a personal stake in it; it is our own lives. We must continue to insist that our elected officials, in meeting their obligations for our security, give arms control at least as high a priority as arms.

American voters would also like to be able to judge leaders on their actual *achievements* in arms reductions. However, it "takes two to tango" and the blame for failure in the end may lie with Soviet leaders or with both parties. Nevertheless, voters can rightly insist that U.S. negotiating efforts and weapons programs provide evidence of a strong commitment to progress in substantive arms control. An arms control movement can also work to build its strength and spread its message abroad. No country, including the Soviet Union, is totally immune to pressures from its friends, its allies, and its population. We must never forget what these weapons do and that what is at stake is the survival of civilization as we know it. Avoiding a nuclear holocaust is our sacred moral obligation to generations yet unborn.

The Imperative of Arms Control

The United States and the Soviet Union have three means available in efforts to reduce and ultimately remove the nuclear sword of Damocles that hangs over us so threateningly: negotiations, restraint, and unilateral initiatives. Negotiations and treaties are crucial in order to identify and confirm areas in which these two superpowers share compatible strategic goals. They provide a framework for progress. But negotiations alone are inadequate, as the record of the past shows. We—meaning both the United States and the Soviet Union—must also exercise restraint, and, where useful, take unilateral steps based on a clear vision of our strategic goals and of what we hope to achieve in our negotiations. Our decisions about weapons programs—which weapons to get rid of, and whether or not to develop and deploy new weapons—must be consistent with our strategic goals.

In the first chapter I argued that this was not the case at the time of SALT I, and I cited the decision to deploy MIRVs extensively as a case in point. Let me review that decision. Our reason for developing a triad of strategic nuclear delivery systems with very different operating characteristics was to establish a secure and reliable retaliatory force. The alert strategic bombers can scramble and escape damage given the information we will have of Soviet attack. The nuclear ballistic missile submarines move silently and invisibly out in the vast oceans, and therefore cannot be attacked. Our land-based ICBMs are loaded into underground silos that were constructed sufficiently hard so that until recently, at least, they were invulnerable to attack. These forces provide us with a secure deterrent.

When the technology of MIRVs first came along, the original justification was to deploy them as an insurance policy against possible, if still unrealized, Soviet ballistic missile defenses. It was argued that the MIRVs would penetrate such hypothetical defenses by overwhelming their firepower with an intense rain of many warheads. When, however, the SALT I treaty of 1972 prohibited the deployment of nationwide ABM defenses, U.S. MIRV programs did not stop, but proceeded full tilt. Why did we do this? We went ahead with MIRVs because we did not have a clear statement and vision of deterrence based on retaliation as our strategic goal. Instead, we implicitly added a requirement for counterforce to our strategic goals without clearly recognizing the inconsistency between mutual deterrence, which is based on secure retaliatory forces for both the United States and the Soviet Union, and a counterforce policy based on extensively deploying a direct threat to the Soviet retaliatory force. As I argued in Chapter 1, you cannot have it both ways. Predictably, Soviet MIRV deployment followed that of the United States four years later and has continued up to the present with considerable—you might even say astonishing—intensity in their SS-18 and SS-19 programs.

The net result is that today, thirteen years after the start of the SALT negotiations designed specifically to limit and reduce the danger of these long-range strategic forces, the United States and the Soviet Union have three times as many deployed nuclear warheads as when we started. The ongoing MX debate shows that we have yet to resolve the confusion in our strategic goals. In the meantime, the danger is growing worse because the weaponeers have been compounding our problems more rapidly than our arms negotiators have been solving them. As Albert Einstein once said, "Politics is much harder than physics."

At the same time that I identify the failures of our past record, I also want to recognize its important successes. The most important success, of course, is that deterrence has worked, and for thirty-eight years since Hiroshima and Nagasaki we have avoided nuclear war. I also chalk up as a major success the fact that the United States and the Soviet Union have demonstrated in the SALT I treaty and the signed but unratified SALT II treaty that we can clearly define our common interests, and on the basis of these common interests negotiate significant and verifiable treaties. Nevertheless, the record is clear that negotiations alone—lacking restraint—are inadequate.

In this chapter I want to identify principles and discuss paths toward achieving in the years ahead what President Eisenhower called, in his famous farewell to the nation at the end of his presidency in 1960, "the continuing imperative" for "disarmament with mutual honor and confidence."

I will speak about nuclear weapons because of the enormity of their destructiveness and of the dangers of nuclear holocaust. And I will start by concentrating on the strategic or intercontinental-range systems that have been the subject of negotiating efforts of SALT (Strategic Arms Limitations Talks) and now START (Strategic Arms Reduction Talks) since 1969.

Arms control—through negotiation, restraint, and unilateral initiatives—is the first step toward reducing and eventually eliminating the nuclear threat. Its value lies in the contribution it makes to our security by reducing the risks of war, and particularly a war with nuclear weapons. Arms control negotiations are concerned with identifying limitations that each party to the negotiations views as contributing to improving its security. These limitations can apply to numbers of selected types of weapons as well as to qualitative changes in their properties. In practice, arms control treaties must be verifiable and negotiations must be specific about agreed means of verification and procedures for making available the information that is required in order to establish treaty compliance. Arms control treaties do not depend on trust. Verification is a particularly important and difficult problem in today's world because of the great difference between the openness of U.S. society and the very secretive nature of the Soviet government.

VERIFICATION

Agreement on the means of verification, along with specified procedures so as not to impede the effectiveness of these means, was an essential achievement of SALT I. The ratified treaty of SALT I commits both nations "not to interfere with the national technical means of verification of the other party." "National technical means" is a euphemism for reconnaissance satellites, which view the world below as they circle 100 or more miles high in the sky, and for technical intelligence collection systems outside national borders. The treaty also stipulates that "each party undertakes not to use deliberate concealment measures which impede verification by national technical means of compliance with the provisions of this Treaty."

The United States and the Soviet Union agree that technology in general and intelligence satellites in particular have made this a more open world where large-scale weapons activities are very difficult, if not impossible, to conceal. Intelligence satellites have pierced the iron curtain and made arms control practical.

In order to monitor U.S. and Soviet compliance with the provisions of the treaty, SALT I created a Standing Consultative Commission: the SCC for short. The SCC meets at least once every six months and provides a regular forum to review events, consider challenges, and resolve ambiguities with respect to compliance with provisions of the treaty. This procedure has been working satisfactorily since its inception in 1972. Verification provisions were further extended in the SALT II negotiations, which culminated in 1979 in a treaty not yet ratified by the United States Senate. In particular, SALT II states that the Soviet Union and the United States will provide figures on their own strategic offensive forces to establish a data base. It also stipulates that missile test firings will be announced and that information from test flights that is essential to verification will not be denied by being encrypted—that is, the relevant telemetry will not be transmitted in code during these tests.

Much emphasis has been placed recently on the importance of improving our ability to verify provisions of arms control agreements. In part, this emphasis is prompted by the advances in weapons technology that are leading to smaller systems—some of which are mobile and some with dual functions—that are harder to keep track of by our reconnaissance satellites alone. An example of this is the cruise missile. In contrast to ballistic missiles, which fly up and out of the atmosphere in their long-range tests, cruise missiles fly low down in the atmosphere and can be programmed on closed trajectories confined well within national borders. Thus their tests are not readily visible. Furthermore, the ability of long-range cruise missiles to be deployed in a dual mode with either nuclear or nonnuclear warheads adds to the ambiguities of what systems to include in any nuclear weapons count.

Another reason for the current emphasis on improved verification stems from concerns about Soviet failure to cooperate and respond to queries about the highly publicized Sverdlovsk incident. As reported, a number of deaths attributed to anthrax occurred there. Apparently these deaths resulted from the release of biological warfare material from a nearby plant. Whether this plant is operating in violation of the Biological Weapons Convention, signed in 1972 and in force since 1975, is not resolved. This is because that convention permits use of such agents for research and for protective purposes, and there can be a range of judgments on what quantities of material would be legitimate. However, the failure of the Soviets to respond in a satisfactory manner to requests for more details on the event is in itself considered by many a violation of the Convention.* Some kind of provision in the Convention for on-site inspection might have helped clarify this incident, but it also raises the question whether either country would permit on-site inspection of sensitive military facilities.

A third reason for renewed emphasis on improving verification derives from interest expressed by the Reagan administration in adding the on-site inspection requirement to current treaties in order to set a precedent for future arms control agreements. For example, the United States now proposes to modify the threshold test ban treaty with the Soviet Union, signed in 1974 and sent to the U.S. Senate in 1976 but not yet ratified. This treaty limits all underground nuclear explosions to a maximum yield of 150 kilotons. It includes a protocol describing the exchange of technical data to improve the accuracy with which the yields of underground explosions can be determined by national technical means—that is, seismic stations outside the United States and the Soviet Union. On this basis it has been argued that adding a requirement of on-site inspection of the test area will be of only marginal value, since it will add little to the accuracy in determining the yield in the test. Nevertheless, it can be viewed as a precedent for future negotiations.

This whole issue of on-site inspection is a very sensitive one to the United States as well as the Soviet Union. For example, it was reported that concern about Soviet inspectors wandering and nosing around our bomb test site in Nevada led to opposition in some

*There is also a growing concern, caused by the evidence for "yellow rain" in Asia, that the Soviet military are not constrained by this Convention.

circles in the U.S. government to adding the on-site inspection requirement to the threshold test ban treaty. It seems to be a rule that no military establishment welcomes intrusive on-site inspection with open arms; and understandably so. On the other hand, on-site inspection would be essential to monitor the production levels at plants producing missiles or weapons-grade nuclear material under any agreement. In this respect a complete production cutoff such as proposed in a comprehensive "freeze" agreement is simpler to monitor and verify.

I would add another caution about verification requirements in general. They can serve as a serious roadblock to progress in arms control if they are applied too rigidly. Or they can compromise our security if applied too carelessly. In negotiating an arms control treaty we must satisfy ourselves, for each provision considered individually, that we can identify any violations that are large enough to endanger our security. In addition, we must be able to establish credible evidence of such violations. This procedure is not entirely free of risks; but then neither is an arms competition without limits. Our goal is to establish a favorable balance of risks, taking into account all of our intelligence resources—technical and human.

Negotiating Goals

Let me turn next to our goals in the arms control negotiations on strategic nuclear weapons, recognizing that the means and requirements of verification put practical limits on what we can actually do.

In Chapter 1, I emphasized the importance of mutual deterrence based on secure retaliatory forces of both the Soviet Union and the United States as offering the best means we know of for avoiding nuclear conflict. This policy also removes incentive for more weapons. Strategic stability, especially during times of heightened tension or in a crisis, is enhanced if both nations are free of the plague of vulnerable systems. This plague is best summed up as the concern "to use them or lose them." Therefore, the first and overriding goal of arms control negotiations should be: *To enhance strategic stability based on a balance of highly survivable and secure deterrent forces.*

I also emphasized in Chapter 1 that nuclear deterrence has serious blemishes. A policy of deterrence should, therefore, be accepted *conditionally* while the United States and the Soviet Union strive to reduce the size of their arsenals as far as possible and thereby reduce the level of devastation if deterrence fails. To this end a second goal of negotiations should be: *To initiate significant, timely, and verifiable reductions in the nuclear forces and destructive potential of both nations.*

Whereas the United States and the Soviet Union may well agree—and hopefully do agree— on those two general goals for a negotiation, we must also accept the realities of today's forces. I emphasized in Chapter 1 that there is, in fact, a rough overall balance between the strategic nuclear forces of the United States and the Soviet Union, although category by category there are great differences. Inevitably, therefore, the two countries will follow very different paths in working to achieve the first two goals of enhanced stability and reductions. Hence the treaty provisions being negotiated should be designed as follows: *To allow the two countries to implement the negotiated provisions by means of selective reductions in accord with their very different technological and bureaucratic styles. While these reductions must be equitable, they may, at the same time, be asymmetric. Thus the negotiations must be highly flexible.*

Finally, it is important for the public to appreciate the value and the equity of an arms control treaty that has been crafted at the negotiating table. Public support can be essential to creating the necessary two-thirds majority vote for ratifying a treaty in the Senate. Therefore, it is very important: *To negotiate a treaty that is conceptually simple so as to be readily explained and comprehended in the broad public debate.*

LIMITING WARHEADS

In order to meet these four goals of enhanced stability, timely reductions, flexibility, and simplicity I recommend that we include a direct limit on the number of nuclear warheads on the long-range bombers and missiles in any future treaty negotiation. This recommendation is a change from the previous approaches of SALT I and II, which directly limited only the number of deployed launchers. In SALT I, the number of missile launchers was frozen at existing levels, including those already under construction; but MIRVing was not restricted. In SALT II, restrictions were added to a number of individual subcategories of missiles. There also were useful constraints on increases in the numbers of warheads that could be added to individual subcategories, but the total number of warheads was allowed to grow substantially. The approach of SALT in the 1970s was effective in putting a ceiling on the number of missile launchers—and this was important (for example, no new ICBM silos have been built since 1972). But this approach has had an undesirable side effect. Since only the launchers are counted, it provided an incentive to build large missiles, each carrying many warheads: witness the modern Soviet missiles, the SS-18 with ten warheads and the SS-19 with six; also the U.S. MX with ten warheads and our submarine-based missile force that is also highly MIRVed.

It is precisely this trend to high fractionation (loading many warheads on individual missiles) that is not good for stability. A large ratio of warheads to launchers creates the fear that only a few of the attacker's missiles can destroy many missiles and many more warheads of his enemy in a first strike. For example, one perfectly operating Soviet SS-18 with its ten warheads might destroy ten U.S. ICBMs in their silos, thereby decreasing our force by 100 warheads if these silos are filled with MX missiles. This postulated 10 to 1 advantage to the Soviets would disappear, of course, if the missiles each carried only one warhead—that is, if there were no MIRVs. In this case each attacking missile with its single warhead could destroy at most one missile and one warhead in a silo. There would be no gain in such an exchange; indeed, the attacker would be worse off after the attack, since he would have to launch extra warheads—up to twice as many in practice— to compensate for failures and aiming errors.

Effectively then, the lower its value, the less vulnerable a system is. This is why I recommend counting the number of warheads and limiting their number directly. With warheads specified as the coin of the realm in the negotiations, we take away the advantage of crowding many MIRVs onto a single missile, because each of the individual warheads would be tallied up under any agreed ceiling.

A provision to count warheads can be verified by national technical means according to the counting rules adopted during the SALT II negotiations. These rules count each missile of a given type, as identified by its external observables and those of its launching silo, as if it carries the same number of warheads as the maximum it has been observed to deliver during its program of test firings. I believe this a reasonable provision because there is, in practice, a very strong disincentive to load more warheads on a missile than have been tested. And national technical means are effective for monitoring tests. I also believe that this is the only practical way to define the count of warheads without requiring unacceptably intrusive practices.

Aside from the number of warheads, there are other numerical measures of the destructive potential that can be used for purposes of counting in a negotiation. These include the volume of the missile and its throw weight (the total weight of warheads and their reentry vehicles plus the post-boost vehicle, or the so-called "bus" for dispensing the MIRVs). Volume and throw weight can be grouped together because they are not very different.

There is nothing wrong with trying to limit throw weight, as many advocate in this country, except that this is probably the fastest way to stop a negotiation dead in its tracks. Throw weight is a parameter that emphasizes maximally to U.S. advantage the disparate technological styles between U.S. and Soviet forces. Put most graphically, the throw weight of the SS-18 is approximately 15,000 pounds; the throw weight of the MX, if we deploy one, would be about half of that. Yet when both are armed with ten warheads, there probably is no military man or strategic planner in the world who would not choose the MX over the SS-18. It is a better missile, with better technology. Therefore, if one tries to construct a counting rule that measures volume or throw weight, thereby making the SS-18 twice as expensive to keep in the Soviet force as the MX is for the United States, the negotiation is not likely to get very far. Whereas throw weight limits might be introduced for future systems in order to decrease the total threatening megatonnage of nuclear weapons, I would view them as an obstacle to current negotiating efforts.

There is also little reason to use megatonnage or throw weight to measure the effectiveness of the present strategic forces. With the aiming accuracies of better than 1,000 feet that can be achieved today, the yield of a weapon is of much less importance than its accuracy against small hardened targets. Against cities, the difference between fractions of megatons and megatons isn't going to matter very much in any event. Overall accuracy is much more important than yield, and the number of warheads is the most effective measurement. By measuring volume, throw weight, or megatonnage, one is, by and large, confusing technological style with force effectiveness.

In the interest of arms control and of balancing the most effective parameter of the weaponry, limiting the number of warheads is a most promising approach. It will enhance stability by providing a strong incentive to reduce preferentially the number of highly MIRVed missiles, which become very expensive to retain under a warhead ceiling. It is highly flexible if each country has the freedom to mix between warheads based on land, on sea, and on aircraft—up to the agreed ceiling on the total force. It is simple and easily understood and explained if both countries are limited by the same total number. It will lead to significant and timely reductions under a suitably negotiated total.

Limits on Testing

Better than reducing numbers alone would be a treaty that sets appropriate qualitative limits that can improve deterrence. These limits should be designed to prevent those force improvements that increase the destructive potential or the counterforce threat of missiles and, at the same time, permit those activities that improve the security of the retaliatory forces. The Carter administration tried such an approach to qualitative limits in its comprehensive proposal of March 1977, which specified a very low quota of six missile test firings per year among its many other provisions. The goal of this restriction on test firings was to head off the development by the Soviet Union and the United States of very high performance missiles with the reliability and accuracy required to pose counterforce threats against each other's ICBM silos. I very much regret—as a number of Russians have also admitted—that the Soviets rejected that approach out of hand on grounds unrelated to the merits of the test firing limit. It would be useful to resurrect this kind of approach, but I suspect that can happen only after we achieve a measure of success with the current efforts based on numerical ceilings. In any event, there is less mileage to be gained from test firing restraints at present than there was in 1977, since it is too late to head off the technology of counterforce. We already have it. Nevertheless, over the long run, qualitative limits can be very useful.*

One very practical form of test restrictions that has been considered for many years is a ban on all underground nuclear explosions. A comprehensive test ban treaty, or CTBT, banning all nuclear bomb tests has been considered for twenty-five years since the Eisenhower administration. The United States and the Soviet Union came close to a comprehensive test ban treaty in 1963, but it got away from us over a difference in verification requirements.

Between 1977 and 1980 the United States, the Soviet Union, and Great Britain negotiated the main elements of a CTBT involving unmanned seismic monitoring stations on the territories of these three nations, plus some procedures for on-site inspection based on a quota of specific challenges for suspicious events. Regrettably, there is no active negotiating effort toward a CTBT at present. Were we to negotiate a CTBT today it would fulfill a commitment that the United States, the Soviet Union, and all the signatories to the atmospheric test ban treaty of 1963 and the nonproliferation treaty of 1970 have made to the other nonnuclear signatories. This evidence of our commitment to control nuclear arms would contribute to strengthening international efforts—and superpower leadership—to

---

*Limits on flight testing of missile systems are a practical and gradual way of implementing a freeze, since new systems can be introduced only very slowly, if at all, under a very restrictive quota of test flights. Another benefit is that severe testing limits will inevitably reduce *confidence* in the ability of both countries to maintain the fine tuning of existing systems to the precision needed for counterforce.

prevent any further spread of nuclear weapons. I believe a CTBT is consistent with maintaining a weapons stockpile whose reliability meets the requirements of deterrence.

THREE PROPOSALS

In the wake of the failure ro ratify SALT II, a number of new approaches to arms control and reductions have emerged. President Reagan's START proposal announced in May 1982 calls for a limit of 5,000 on the number of missile warheads and a separate one of 850 on the missiles. In addition, it stipulates that at least half of the 5,000 permitted warheads and 850 launchers must be at sea; hence no more than half can be on land. It puts no limits on the slow-flying systems—bombers and their armaments of gravity bombs and cruise missiles—although these systems are identified as candidates for a separate negotiation. Finally, it proposes to include throw-weight limits in a later stage of negotiations.

The main virtues of the Reagan proposal are that it calls for significant and balanced reductions by both countries and it focuses directly on numbers of warheads. But it also has three basic difficulties: (1) By stipulating a ceiling with so large a ratio of warheads to launchers (5,000/850, or almost 6 to 1), it does not improve stability. If anything, it is a step in the wrong direction, because it allows—and encourages—the ratio of warheads to launchers to increase rather than to decrease from current values. (2) By insisting that at least half the deployments be at sea, it lacks the necessary flexibility. In particular, it mandates a major change in the technological style of the Soviets away from their land-based rocket forces, in which they have made a huge investment, and requires them to mirror our strength as a sea power in spite of their limited access to oceans. (3) By deferring the bomber component, it leaves unrestricted a force in which our technological edge is pronounced, and growing with our deployment of long-range air-launched cruise missiles.

In Senate testimony* I gave in January 1982, I proposed a related but different approach of adding up all the strategic systems—the intercontinental missiles and bombers—and setting an overall ceiling on the number of launchers plus warheads together, instead of separately. In particular I suggested a ceiling of 8,000, which is little more than half of the ceiling for which we now have programs under way. By specifying this single numerical ceiling of 8,000 we can achieve the four desired objectives: TIMELY REDUCTIONS: The United States and the Soviet Union will have to reduce their forces by about 20 percent under their current deployments. SIMPLICITY: This is evident. In particular by fixing only the total we avoid the complexities of comparing very different systems and having to make the kinds of compromises in these comparisons that made SALT II so vulnerable politically. MAXIMUM FLEXIBILITY: The United States and the Soviet Union would be free to choose their own paths to reductions without being forced to change their technological styles to accommodate each other's strengths and weaknesses. IMPROVED STABILITY: Each country would selectively reduce the highly MIRVed systems that become so expensive in the count.

* Published in the *Bulletin of the Atomic Scientists*, April 1982.

There are several reasons that led me to include the number of launchers plus the number of warheads in this proposal. Two in particular are: (1) It provides some continuity with the past negotiating record, a fact of considerable political value. (2) Including launchers in the count severely limits any possibilities for using this approach to build up a launcher number greatly in excess of currently negotiated ceilings. I gave additional arguments of a more technical nature in support of this variant of a warhead ceiling. They are not of great importance. The more important point to emphasize is that there is little difference between limiting warheads plus launchers and a straight ceiling on warheads alone. Both schemes create pressures to de-MIRV the forces but remain flexible by not demanding it. Whichever counting scheme is more negotiable is the one that should be pursued. But under no circumstance should we become too literally bound by fascination with numbers alone. We need more boldness in seeking arms control progress, more common sense in emphasizing the function of our weapons, and less detailed balancing of numbers.

In this discussion I have so far focused on putting ceilings on the number of deployed warheads and systems. If such a treaty can be negotiated, we will have legislated a limit to our "appetite" for nuclear warheads for our strategic systems. It then becomes both attractive and feasible to consider means of reducing the amount of weapons-grade fissionable material, which is the "food supply" for satisfying that appetite. A limit on both the appetite and the food supply would indeed be a very powerful approach to effective arms control.

A "supply-side" proposal of this kind dates back all the way to the Eisenhower administration. It has recently been put forward again by the American Committee on East-West Accord, spearheaded by retired Admiral Noel Gayler, former Commander in Chief, Pacific Forces (CINCPAC), director of the National Security Agency, and strategic planner during a most distinguished naval career. This proposal would achieve deep cuts by the following combination of three steps to be taken by the United States and the Soviet Union: (1) Turn in nuclear weapons and convert their fissionable material to fuel for nuclear power plants. (2) Halt the production of weapons-grade material. (3) Agree to full-scope safeguards covering the entire nuclear fuel cycle to prevent diversion of material to weapons.

This is a true "swords into plowshares" proposal that meets all of the desirable criteria for arms control: It is simple. It can lead to timely reductions. It is flexible, since each country chooses the weapons to turn in according to its own needs and desires. It will inevitably improve stability, since the most likely weapons to go are those that currently are most dangerous—the old and numerous battlefield weapons that are so close to the front lines and the highly MIRVed systems. Both are basically heavy eaters, or hogs, of nuclear material.

Furthermore, this is a verifiable proposal. The required on-site inspection will not involve intrusion into militarily significant technology. Let me amplify this point a bit. In order to monitor the turning in of weapons, one need only take a low-quality X ray of a device at a neutral site without requiring intrusive detailed inspection. It is then left to nationals of each country to disfigure the device mechanically. The total weight of fissionable material turned in can be weighed and turned over to a designated authority to rule out any diversion into the hands of third parties. This step requires no compromise of military technology.

The second step in this proposal of halting production of weapons-grade material and the third one of preventing diversion from power reactors will require safeguards to be imposed on the entire nuclear fuel cycle—the production reactors, enrichment plants, and plutonium reprocessing plants if any are in operation. The precedent for this has been set by the International Atomic Energy Agency (IAEA) in Vienna: the experience exists already. The appropriate authority to manage these steps, if not the IAEA, can be determined in due course. The procedures will be as good as our support of them—with enough inspectors and access. They can meet, but are not required to, the exacting and severe standards imposed today under the nonproliferation treaty. This is because a relatively small error that permits a nonnuclear nation to become a nuclear nation with one or a few bombs doesn't really matter when we're talking about 25,000 or so, which is today's starting point, given the arsenals of the United States and Soviet Union.*

* A side benefit of this cutoff of the nuclear food supply is its contribution to our ability to put effective limits on deployment of some of the newer weapons that are more difficult to verify by national technical means alone. I have in mind, in particular, the force of the new sea-launched cruise missiles designed with a dual capability to carry nonnuclear as well as nuclear warheads—the former for war at sea and the latter for a land attack and as a so-called strategic reserve force. These new weapons will be avaricious consumers of weapons-grade material if deployed in large

In our efforts to reduce weapons and to reduce the risks of nuclear conflict we must also address the problems posed by the shorter-range nuclear forces. These include the intermediate-range nuclear forces, or INF, in Europe and many thousands of battlefield nuclear weapons that are only seconds or minutes from hitting targets, or being hit. They are very dangerous as triggers of conflict.

We are currently negotiating with the Russians—so far without much promise of success—in an effort to reduce the threat posed by both of these forces. The INF talks, which are concerned with nuclear missiles and aircraft in Europe whose ranges are characteristically between 1,000 and 3,000 miles, were initiated as a result of two developments: (1) The growth of a Soviet strategic forces to a rough parity with those of the United States. It was expected that a SALT II treaty would formally recognize this parity. (2) The growing deployment of the Soviets' new SS-20 intermediate-range ballistic missiles which are mobile, accurate, and MIRVed with three warheads.

It was perceived by the leaders of the NATO countries that these developments required a reponse. In particular it was claimed by Europeans that the U.S. strategic forces—in an era of parity—were no longer an effective deterrent to Soviet aggression against them. Their fear was quite simply that we would not risk our people and cities for Europe. Thus it became a

---

numbers. A lowering of the material supply will pose an effective limit on their deployment, and this will enhance the usual means of counting.

matter of alliance solidarity for the United States to couple its nuclear deterrent more tightly to Europe by introducing missiles on the continent in order to balance the growing SS-20 missile threat.

These concerns led NATO to take a two-track decision in December 1979, which was hoped to prevent further growth of nuclear forces in Europe. The first track was to negotiate to reduce and remove the still growing threat of ground-launched missiles in Europe. The second track was to begin preparations for deploying U.S. ground-launched cruise missiles and extended-range Pershing II ballistic missiles starting by the end of 1983 if the first, or negotiating, track failed.

When the actual negotiations on INF began in Geneva on November 30, 1981, both the United States and the Soviet Union adopted extreme opening positions. Out of one corner came the Soviet Union with the proposal to add no more missiles following their buildup of some 300 SS-20s with 900 warheads—if the West does nothing. Out of the opposite corner came the United States saying it will forgo its planned deployment of 572 missiles in Europe if the Soviets dismantle all their comparable missiles of intermediate range, that is, their SS-4s, 5s, and 20s. Just as the Soviet proposal is lopsided in that it confirms a *fait accompli,* the U.S. proposal is lopsided in that it focuses only on the intermediate-range land-based missiles in which the Soviets have concentrated their strength. But it leaves untouched all other systems of Western strength, including our Poseidon ships assigned to the Supreme Allied Commander for Europe, our long-range nuclear-armed aircraft, and the British-French national forces of 162 missiles that threaten the Soviet heartland. Certainly a compromise between these two opening gambits is required.

I welcome the fact that both the United States and the Soviet Union have recently backed off from their quite unrealistic opening positions, thereby improving prospects for success of these negotiations. But there remain very major differences to resolve between the two sides and there is a severe time pressure for making progress, because the scheduled date for NATO to start deploying its missiles is December 1983. The two most serious problems remaining to be resolved are: (1) The difference between Soviet insistence on "equal security" versus U.S. insistence on "equal numbers." In other words, how does one implicitly, if not explicitly, compensate for the 162 missiles under national control of the French and the British. (2) The question of which systems to include in the count, in addition to ground-based missiles in Europe, in order to achieve an equitable balance. In particular, which long-range aircraft and sea-based systems are counted, and which missiles in other global regions as emphasized in recent U.S. statements.

One way to diminish the significance of these differences would be to combine the INF and the strategic, or START, talks and seek a single agreement with an overall limit on all U.S. and Soviet nuclear systems having a range of 1,000 miles or longer. This includes the Soviets SS-4s, 5s, and 20s, U.S. cruise and Pershing II missiles, and many aircraft on both sides. There are two arguments for such a merger: (1) The numerical impact of the British-French systems and of exactly which aircraft are or are not included in the count is only a small fraction of the grand total of intermediate- and intercontinental-range warheads and launchers. Therefore, it should be easier to negotiate the necessary compromises, since they involve forces that represent only a small percentage of the total. (2) Limits on the long range threater nuclear forces make much more sense when there are also limits on the strategic forces. After all, what matters is not where the missile takes off, but where it comes down! In fact, it was assumed that there would be a ratified SALT II agreement by now when NATO made its two-track decision in 1979.

A specific form for this merger would be to set a single numerical ceiling on the launchers plus warheads of all systems of 1,000-mile range and longer. Under this ceiling each country would have freedom to design whatever mix of forces it chooses. Earlier I discussed a proposal to set a ceiling of 8,000 for the number of launchers plus warheads on the strategic systems alone, arguing this number to be roughly half the presently planned total. Using the same logic, I have proposed* a combined INF and START total of 9,000. There is no magic to this number. I used it in my Senate testimony only to present an extremely simple and valuable approach in its most conservative form. This proposal can also be used as a specific means to implement George Kennan's suggestion in 1981 to cut in half *existing* forces instead of the planned ones as I did in my example. This would leave an overall launcher

---

* See the earlier reference to my Senate testimony of January 1982 (published in the *Bulletin of the Atomic Scientists*).

plus warhead total of about 6,000—more than enough. Reductions to this total would be a truly bold and great move, although for starters I'd be happy with the 9,000 figure. We mustn't forget that at some level the other nuclear armed nations would have to become partners in the process.

Finally, we have to face the problem of what to do with all those battlefield nuclear weapons—the artillery shells, short-range rockets and missiles, demolition mines, and the like that are deployed only short distances and fleeting moments from the front lines in Europe and at other areas of potential confrontation around the world. The greatest danger of nuclear weapons lies not in their accumulation but in the possibility that they might actually be used through mistake, miscalculation, or misunderstanding. In this regard, many would agree that it is the thousands of battlefield weapons—with their long and tenuous lines of command authority from Moscow and from Washington—that pose the greatest threat. Current NATO doctrine provides no grounds for comfort. The U.S. Army's Field Manual 100-5 recognizes and describes the circumstances of introducing these battlefield nuclear weapons into a conflict in Europe in order to repulse a Warsaw Pact thrust to the West with conventional forces. But what about the danger of ensuing escalation to a nuclear holocaust amid the confusion, the errors, and the technical failures of the battlefield? NATO should not be relying on its battlefield nuclear weapons as a crutch to compensate for inadequacies in the conventional forces. It is too dangerous a policy. Indeed, would anything be left of Europe after a nuclear war was waged to save it?

Toward Nuclear Disengagement

We should remove all battlefield nuclear weapons—
and along with them the dangerous fantasy of current
NATO doctrine. Last year the Soviet Union officially
affirmed a change in its policy and announced a doctrine of "no first use" of nuclear weapons. I heard a
very strong presentation of this change from a senior
general on the Soviet general staff when I was in Moscow in December 1982. In addition, the Soviet military has rewritten army manuals to reflect that change.
Such declarations and words are welcome—and not
without value as a signal of Soviet thinking and inten-
tions. Of course, actions and evidence of actual military preparations are of considerably greater value.

For NATO, the first step of a real nuclear disengagement must be the maintenance of a conventionally
armed force by the alliance nations that is adequate for
the defense of Western Europe. This does not require a
big military buildup, although some have attempted
to portray the requirements for a conventional defense
of Europe in such terms. We could pay for our share
with a modest reprogramming of existing defense dollars from our gold-plated nuclear programs—such as
MX, B-1B, and new nuclear aircraft carriers—to the
conventional forces, with appropriate emphasis given
to the newest technology of precision-guided munitions. General Bernard Rogers, Supreme Allied Commander in Europe, recently estimated the requirements for an adequate conventional defense of Europe
at no more than about 1 to 1.5 percent beyond presently planned programs for the alliance.

Progress in the MBFR (mutual and balanced force reduction) talks in Vienna that have dragged on for more than a decade could decrease these costs. An agreement there to redeploy battlefield nuclear weapons farther back from the front lines and to create a nuclear free zone in Europe would also be an important step toward nuclear disengagement. But we shouldn't wait for those developments. Here, if anywhere, is a prime area for bold unilateral action by the United States. We should simply begin removing some of these dangerous weapons of which there are currently 6,000 in our European arsenal. There is a precedent for such action. We reduced this arsenal from 7,000 to 6,000 in 1979, and the same year the Soviets withdrew 20,000 troops and 1,000 tanks. It matters not that these were not weapons or troops of top quality. It was a constructive action. We need more bold, unilateral actions of that sort.

In order to expedite such actions we should also engage in discussions leading to improved cooperation at the military level, including more communication between staff and the presence of observers, especially during maneuvers. These are actions that come under the heading of confidence-building and crisis-avoidance measures and are, I believe, practical. They are often advocated by both sides in discussions with colleagues from Moscow, but they need implementation.

I consider them the necessary prelude if we are effectively to back off from current doctrines that imply early first use, and to take instead a position of no early first use of nuclear weapons. Our eventual goal should be a policy of no use—first, second, or third, or at any level. When dealing with weapons of suicide there are no sensible way stations. Sanity is synonomous with no use whatever.

There are also no sensible way stations—or comfort stops—along the negotiating route short of the goal endorsed by President Reagan when he said that he would "negotiate as long as necessary to reduce the numbers of nuclear weapons to a point where neither side threatens the survival of the other." His emphasis on negotiating our way out from the nuclear threat is well placed, but I would welcome more convincing evidence of actions by his administration.

On March 23, 1983, President Reagan also proposed that we turn to space-age technology in order to counter the nuclear threat to our survival with a defensive umbrella. I believe there is more "pie in the sky" than realism in that proposal, which I will discuss in chapter 3. In search of security I know of no technological alternative to the imperative of arms control. George Kennan stated it elegantly and forcefully in his new book, *The Nuclear Delusion*, in words that summarize this chapter:

> Whoever does not understand that when it comes to nuclear weapons the whole concept of relative advantage is illusory—whoever does not understand that when you are talking about absurd and preposterous quantities of overkill the relative sizes of arsenals have no serious meaning—whoever does not understand that the danger lies, not in the possibility that someone else might have more missiles and warheads than we do, but in the very existence of these unconscionable quantities of highly poisonous explosives,

and their existence, above all, in hands as weak and shaky and undependable as those of ourselves or our adversaries or any other mere human beings: whoever does not understand these things is never going to guide us out of this increasingly dark and menacing forest of bewilderments into which we have all wandered.

I can see no way out of this dilemma other than by a bold and sweeping departure, a departure that would cut surgically through the exaggerated anxieties, the self-engendered nightmares, and the sophisticated mathematics of destruction in which we have all been entangled over these recent years, and would permit us to move, with courage and decision, to the heart of the problem.*

*George F. Kennan, *The Nuclear Delusion: Soviet-American Relations in the Atomic Age* (New York: Pantheon Books, 1982).

The Scientist's Dilemma

The Faustian Bargain

Early in the nineteenth century Goethe made the Faust legend into so great a work of literature that it has permeated Western culture. We have all become familiar with the fate of the scholar who left his ivory tower and made a pact with the devil, to whom he mortgaged his soul.

Today—as often in history—the scientist is lured from his laboratory into the outer world by the attraction of power and influence, and sometimes by challenging technical opportunities, and often finds, like Faust, that the experience is painful as well as bewildering. Trained to study the fixed and rational laws of nature, the scientist, once he leaves his laboratory, encounters in the outer world the shifting and often apparently irrational laws of political and social interactions. In a sense, like Faust, he has sold his soul to the devil; and the end is often disillusion.

There is, however, a new twist to this circumstance today, and it puts a heavy burden on scientists—individually and collectively. This new circumstance was emphasized by C. P. Snow in the opening paragraphs of his famous Godkin Lectures on "Science and Government," which he gave at Harvard University in

1960 (published by Harvard University Press, 1961).
Snow began his lectures thus:

> One of the most bizarre features of any advanced industrial society in our time is that the cardinal choices have to be made by a handful of men: in secret; and, at least in legal form, by men who cannot have a firsthand knowledge of what those choices depend upon or what their results may be.
>
> When I say "advanced industrial society" I am thinking in the first place of the three in which I am most interested—the United States, the Soviet Union, and my own country. And when I say the "cardinal choices," I mean those which determine in the crudest sense whether we live or die. For instance, the choice in England and the United States in 1940 and 1941, to go ahead with work on the fission bomb: the choice in 1945 to use that bomb when it was made: the choice in the United States and the Soviet Union, in the late forties, to make the fusion bomb: the choice, which led to a different result in the United States and the Soviet Union, about intercontinental missiles.
>
> It is in the making of weapons of absolute destruction that you can see my central theme at its sharpest and most dramatic, or most melodramatic if you like.

It is precisely "the making of weapons of absolute destruction" that presents a new dilemma to scientists, and to society as well. The involvement of scientists in war and weapons of death is in itself nothing new. Archimedes designed fortifications and instruments of war including a great catapult to help thwart the Romans besieging Syracuse in the third century B.C. Leonardo da Vinci was renowned as one of the greatest military scientists of his time. Lord Solly Zuckerman writes in his recent book *Nuclear Illusion and Reality* (New York: Viking Press, 1982): "The letter which [Leonardo] wrote to Ludovico Sforza, the ruler of the principality of Milan, offering to provide any instruments of war which he could desire—military bridges, mortars, mines, chariots, catapults, and 'other machines of marvellous efficacy not in common use'—was that of an arms salesman, the sort of offer which a later generation might have regarded as emanating from a 'merchant of death.'" Michelangelo at one point during his career was the engineer in chief of the fortifications of Florence. So there is a very distinguished honor roll of scientists who have designed and built weapons.

But never before have scientists dealt with "weapons of absolute destruction," with weapons whose use could mean the end of civilization as we know it—if not of mankind itself. And never before has the gulf been so great between the scientific arguments—even the very language of science—and the political leaders whose decisions will shape the future.

The dilemma of the scientist is heightened greatly by our knowledge that the fruits of our learning now threaten the existence of all mankind. The fact that there is little—precious little if any—room for failure, or margin of safety, emphasizes the precarious predicament of all mankind. This fact mandates that society make optimal use of its scientific and technical resources in order to meet successfully the nuclear challenge. In this circumstance it is vital to bridge the gulf between the two cultures of C. P. Snow. Faust had a choice. Individuals today also have a choice, and as always it is wise for each of us to emphasize our strengths in making that choice. But the two communities as a whole, science and government, have no choice. We must sup together. We are bound tightly by the same grave danger.

I will confine my remarks here to the danger of nuclear holocaust, but there are other scientific areas, such as genetic engineering and environmental changes, where the advancing frontiers of knowledge have given us unprecedented powers to alter the human condition and, as a result, have caused alarm.

THE OPPENHEIMER SAGA

J. Robert Oppenheimer is the best known example of a scientist in recent times who was lured away from his laboratory to build weapons, only to end up disillusioned by the results of his success, and wounded by the society he served so well. Oppenheimer and his colleagues at Los Alamos were the elite of the scientific world, united in their commitment to build an atomic bomb by their fear that Hitler would acquire one from his scientific community. Their elation at the success of their efforts was tempered by uncertainty at the wisdom and necessity of the use of the bomb in the closing stages of World War II following Germany's defeat. As the postwar political climate chilled in a cold war with the Soviet Union, Oppenheimer and many of his colleagues were distressed at the prospects of our moving ahead to the second generation of nuclear weapons. These were the thermonuclear bombs—what we call today hydrogen bombs—for which the fission weapons, or the so-called atom bombs, of Hiroshima and Nagasaki were mere triggers. And with the ashes, the rubble, and the horror of Hiroshima and Nagasaki fresh in their minds the atomic scientists sought ways and means to avert yet another factor of 1,000 growth in the devastating power of weapons.

Oppenheimer was chairman of the General Advisory Committee of the Atomic Energy Commission, which advised the Commission and President Truman on the matter of proceeding to develop the hydrogen bomb. His 1949 report to Commission chairman, David Lilienthal, on behalf of the entire committee includes the following recommendations and concerns (as quoted in York, *The Advisors*):

> It is clear that the use of this weapon would bring about the destruction of innumerable human lives; it is not a weapon which can be used exclusively for the destruction of material installations of military or semi-military purposes. Its use therefore carries much further than the atomic bomb itself the policy of exterminating civilian populations.
>
> We are all reluctant to see the United States take the initiative in precipitating this development. We are all agreed that it would be wrong at the present moment to commit ourselves to an all-out effort toward its development.

After further discussing the nature of the commitment not to develop the weapon, the report continues: "The Committee recommends that enough be declassified about the super bomb so that a public statement of policy can be made at this time."

In an addendum to this report written by James Conant on behalf of the majority of the Committee, including Oppenheimer, the alarms and moral concerns ring out strongly and clearly:

> We are alarmed as to the possible global effects of the radioactivity generated by the explosion of a few super bombs of conceivable magnitude. If super bombs will work at all, there is no inherent limit in the destructive power that may be attained with them. Therefore, a super bomb might become a weapon of genocide.
>
> We believe a super bomb should never be produced. Mankind would be far better off not to have a demonstration of the feasibility of such a weapon until the present climate of world opinion changes.
>
> In determining not to proceed to develop the super bomb, we see a unique opportunity of providing by example some limitations on the totality of war and thus of limiting the fear and arousing the hopes of mankind.

But there was no public debate at that time, and we went ahead with the hydrogen bomb. In the end, Oppenheimer's questioning of the morality of developing the hydrogen bomb was one of the factors which led to his public disgrace as a security risk. For his pact with the devil Oppenheimer ended up both disillusioned and personally devastated.

The Sakharov Saga

Less well known is the career of Andrei D. Sakharov. It epitomizes in its entirety the dilemma of the scientist who makes his Faustian pact. Let me use Sakharov's own words, as taken from his introduction to the book *Sakharov Speaks*. This book, which appeared in 1974, is the first published collection of his writings on social and political issues.*

Sakharov tells of his initial involvement in the Soviet hydrogen bomb project, motivated by his conviction that the world would be safer if there were a socialist bomb to balance a capitalist one: "A few months after defending my dissertation for the degree of Candidate of Doctor of Science, roughly equivalent to an American Ph.D., which occurred in the spring of 1948, I was included in a research group working on the problem of a thermonuclear weapon. I had no doubts as to the vital importance of creating a Soviet superweapon—for our country and for the balance of power throughout the world. Carried away by the immensity of the tasks, I worked very strenuously and became the author or co-author of several key ideas."

In fact, the importance of Sakharov's contribution led to his election as a full member of the Soviet Academy of Sciences at the unprecedented young age of thirty-two, to his receiving many of the highest awards

---

Sakharov Speaks, ed. Harrison E. Salisbury (New York: Alfred A. Knopf, 1974).

and prizes in the Soviet Union, and to his deserved reputation as father of the Soviet hydrogen bomb.

During the 1950s Sakharov writes of becoming increasingly involved with a military-industrial complex "blind to everything except their jobs," and he tells of coming "to reflect in general terms on the problems of peace and mankind and, in particular, on the problems of a thermonuclear war and its aftermath." His concern about the harmful effects of radioactive fallout from atmospheric testing of nuclear bombs led Sakharov to begin a campaign to halt or limit testing. He tells of speaking out in an unsuccessful effort to halt the series of 1958 tests. When in 1961, after a three-year moratorium, the Soviets began preparing for their 1961 test series, Sakharov wrote a note to Khrushchev saying: "To resume tests after a three-year moratorium would undermine the talks on banning tests and on disarmament and would lead to a new round in the armaments race—especially in the sphere of intercontinental missiles and anti-missile defence."

As Sakharov describes it, Khrushchev responded in an off-the-cuff after-dinner speech as follows: "Sakharov is a good scientist. But leave it to us, who are specialists in this tricky business, to make foreign policy." He went on to say: "I would be a slob, and not chairman of the Council of Ministers, if I listened to the likes of Sakharov."

Sakharov tells of "the feelings of impotence and fright that seized" him when he failed to stop a very powerful and technically useless test explosion—and concludes he was deliberately misled by Khrushchev. But there is also the satisfaction he expresses because he was able to use his position in 1962 to present to a key Soviet official an important idea that a friend had told him, which may have been instrumental in bringing about Soviet agreement to the limited test ban treaty of 1963. This treaty banned all but underground tests, thereby removing the hazard of radioactive fallout. Like Oppenheimer, Sakharov was disturbed by the moral consequences and the political use made of his work. Like Faust's, the end of Sakharov's pact with the devil was disillusion. Today his disillusion is total. Exiled to Gorky, and isolated from friends and scientific colleagues, Sakharov continues to caution us about the dangers of nuclear holocaust, as he did in the *New York Times Magazine* on June 8, 1980: "Despite all that has happened, I feel that the questions of war and peace and disarmament are so crucial that they must be given absolute priority even in the most difficult circumstances. It is imperative that all possible means be used to solve these questions and to lay the groundwork for further progress. Most urgent of all are steps to avert a nuclear war, which is the greatest peril confronting the modern world. The goals of all responsible people in the world coincide in this regard, including, I hope and believe, the Soviet leaders...."*

It is now forty years since Oppenheimer and colleagues went to work to build weapons of unparalleled destructive power out of fear of Hitler's Germany. It is thirty-five years since the young Sakharov pitched in to

*In May 1983 I received an open letter from Sakharov summarizing his views on arms control and the threat of nuclear weapons, which are in general very similar to my own. However, Sakharov and I differ on an important issue—the MX missile. Sakharov's letter, which appeared in the summer 1983 issue of *Foreign Affairs*, is reprinted in this volume (see p. 93). My own views on the MX are given in the Appendix.

build a socialist hydrogen bomb to balance a capitalist bomb, and, as he then saw it, contribute to peace and stability through deterrence. In the end they both were bitterly disillusioned and officially outcast. But given the political circumstances at the time of their decisions, and without the benefit of hindsight, who can say that they didn't make the right choice?

As scientists we are trained in, we are expert in, and we work in a field whose content is without moral values, such as the study of the laws and the building blocks of physical nature. But as human beings we must make a moral choice whether or how to involve ourselves with the devil—the political process, government, and weapons of war. Now, however, with nuclear weapons, the fruits of our labors and the consequences of failure of policy may be irreversible for all mankind. It is a very troubling dilemma. In contrast, Leonardo and others were merely dabbling when their actions are viewed on a global scale.

THE IMPORTANCE OF A PUBLIC CONSTITUENCY

The tales of Oppenheimer and Sakharov also illustrate the problems of society—the public—who will be the targets of a nuclear war but are often separated by a veil of secrecy from the fateful decisions being made. Recalling the words of C. P. Snow in his Godkin Lectures, this is "one of the most bizarre features of any advanced industrial society." I also view it as one of our most troubling. At issue is how to have informed debate on basic issues of policy and at the same time protect technical secrets that are directly important to our military effectiveness and intelligence collection.

There was no public debate at the time of the fateful decision by President Truman in 1950 to develop the second generation of nuclear weapons—that is, the H-bomb, or hydrogen bomb. The debate within government on whether, and then how, to proceed with work on the H-bomb in response to the first Soviet A-bomb explosion in late summer of 1949 was carried on almost completely under a thick cloak of secrecy. In the political climate of those days, the United States viewed the Soviet Union as a mortal enemy and secrecy was applied broadly. Remember that this was early in the cold war period. As a result, the public played no role in the decision to move ahead to the megaton H-bomb. There were also no diplomatic initiatives with the Soviets that might have headed off another fateful round of weapons competition. To be sure, there were voices in government urging that we consider a serious negotiating effort to establish international controls of atomic energy before taking the fateful step to the H-bomb. For example, I quote George Kennan's *Memoirs, 1925-1950* (Boston: Little, Brown, 1967): "A number of us, including the late Robert Oppenheimer, felt that before proceeding with the development of weapons of a wholly new range of destructiveness, we should reexamine our situation with respect to the international control of atomic weapons generally, and make sure that there was really no possibility of arriving at international agreements that would obviate the need to embark upon this fateful course." But these voices were to no avail.

The negotiating initiative Kennan was suggesting would have been quite different from the Baruch-Lilienthal plan to put atomic weapons and energy under international control immediately following World War II. The Baruch-Lilienthal plan would have extended a U.S. monopoly in atomic know-how. By way of contrast, what Kennan, Oppenheimer, and others were advocating four years later in 1949 was an agreement to head off the H-bomb development that neither country had yet undertaken or knew how to achieve. What the scientists themselves did know very well, however, was the enormous potential of an H-bomb for devastation and genocide. And indeed many—including pro H-bomb scientists—expressed their hope it could not be built. Nevertheless, the United States and the Soviet Union entered another round of arms competition—in secrecy and without a serious diplomatic initiative either to head it off or, more creatively, if less likely, to move from arms competition to cooperation in peaceful applications such as fusion power to the benefit of both countries and all the world. It was nine years later before a serious initiative on peaceful uses of nuclear energy was made in 1958—but by then it was too late. The genie was out of the bottle and there was no way to deny the basic scientific reality of the hydrogen bomb.

Did we learn from the lost opportunity? As occurs so often in the affairs of mankind, the record is mixed and the answer is "yes in part but not well enough, or rapidly enough."

By the early 1960s the design and building of hydrogen bombs had advanced to a mature technology. The scientists in the nuclear weapons laboratories had become what Lord Zuckerman calls "the alchemists of our time, working in secret ways that cannot be divulged, casting spells which embrace us all." I presume that the alchemists of these weapons were motivated in much the same way as Oppenheimer in 1943 and Sakharov in 1948. But a new element was introduced by 1960, and that was a strong public outcry against the health hazards caused by radioactive fallout from nuclear explosions in the atmosphere. A new coalition was forged in this country and among many peoples around the world on whom the deadly radioactivity descended indiscriminately like the wind-driven snow. An active and vigorous public constituency concerned about the health of their families and friends joined scientists who understood the weapons in detail, and therefore could bring a highly informed judgment to bear on the question of how the cessation of nuclear tests in the atmosphere would affect our national security. This was a very powerful coalition and resulted in the limited test ban treaty signed in 1963 by President Kennedy and Chairman Khrushchev.

This was the first important issue of nuclear weapons in which the public in this country played a major role. I know of no similar public pressure in the Soviet Union when Sakharov and some of his colleagues were also advocating a test ban treaty in 1961 and 1962. In the Western world, however, an extraordinary coalition of concerned citizens by the tens and hundreds of thousands applied strong political leverage at the same time the technical case in support of an atmospheric test ban treaty was presented by concerned scientists. These forces "inside" and "outside" of government enhanced one another. Working together, they helped accomplish what may well have been beyond the power of either alone.

By the end of the 1960s, scientists had developed

important new weapons technologies with the potential to alter in a fundamental way the nuclear forces of the United States and Soviet Union. One new development was ballistic missile defenses, or ABM systems, using advanced computers, very high acceleration interceptor missiles, special nuclear warheads, and phased array radars. The other development was the MIRVs that turned each of our intercontinental missiles into hydra-headed monsters.

The original proposal to deploy ABM systems in the United States near large population centers stirred a major public debate primarily because many people objected to nuclear weapons being introduced, figuratively speaking, "into their own backyards." Triggered by these public concerns, the ABM decision became an opportunity for extensive public debate. The halls of Congress and the media became vital educational forums for careful and informed technical analysis of the effectiveness and arms control implications of the proposed ABM system. By 1970 it was clear on the basis of technical facts alone that Soviet offensive missiles could respond with relative ease to any practical ABM system. The preponderance of offense over defense in the nuclear weapons era is a simple consequence of their enormous destructive power. After careful scrutiny of the countermeasures that could defeat the ABM system, technical arguments for deploying it collapsed and the ABM debate boiled down to its value solely as political leverage for the arms control talks—its value as a bargaining chip for SALT. The Russians faced the same problems for their ABM plans, and furthermore both countries recognized that a major ABM program would stimulate a continuing major buildup of offensive forces by the opponent. The outcome of the review that was initiated by public expressions of concern was the ABM treaty of SALT I, which is currently in force and which I consider to be our most important arms control achievement to date.

At the same time as the ABM debate, the United States moved ahead rapidly with MIRVs. From a technical point of view MIRVs were a natural step to take. There was no technical question about being able to do it. What is more, MIRVs did not lead to an increase in the visible presence of nuclear weapons. Therefore, in contrast to ABMs they did not cause a reaction from citizens who wanted no nuclear weapons nearby. In such circumstances we deployed MIRVs with very little public attention or concern; and as I discussed in my first chapter, arms control and deterrence lost. It is not that there was no opportunity for serious public debate about the pros and cons of MIRVs and their impact on the arms race and our national security. It was simply that there was no specific issue to bring the MIRV decision home to the man in the street and arouse public reaction. Therefore, no public constituency was created to nurture the cause of arms control and deterrence in opposition to the MIRV. Moreover, the country was becoming increasingly concerned first with Vietnam and then with Watergate.

There was also very little expressed public interest in the SALT II treaty when it came up for ratification by the U.S. Senate in 1979. The experts and a few politicians pitched in and argued mightily. However, there was no public outcry as there had been at the time of the ABM debate that set the stage for SALT I. The Senate debate on SALT II dragged on with very little public pressure for ratification and was eventually terminated when the international situation soured for the United States.

I see a pattern in this mixed record of the past. The atmospheric test ban treaty and the ABM debate that culminated in SALT I are two major successes in our nuclear weapons policy. It is notable that they were achieved with vigorous and constructive public participation and support.

On the other hand, the development of the H-bomb and of MIRVs greatly increased the devastating potential and the threat posed by our nuclear weapons. As such they may be considered failures of our nuclear weapons policy. I find it significant that these technical advances were undertaken without public involvement or debate, and also without a serious effort at negotiating them away. When I add to that record the failure to ratify SALT II, I find the evidence persuasive that an active, politically effective, and constructive public constituency is a necessary component for making progress in arms control and reducing the nuclear threat. And that is why I strongly support the freeze movement. Whatever its pros and cons as literal policy, the freeze has helped arouse the public and create an arms control constituency; and the past record shows that the instincts of the public on issues of life and death and nuclear weaponry are pretty good. These instincts expressed themselves through concerns about the harm to our families and friends due to fallout from continued atmospheric testing of nuclear weapons. This was more an environmental than an arms control concern, but it worked in creating the public support for the atmospheric test ban treaty in 1963. It was bombs in the backyard, not a deep issue of deterrence and arms control, that aroused the public and triggered the debate that culminated in the SALT I treaty.

THE "STAR WARS" DEFENSE

Our current freeze-grown arms control constituency faces a busy and very important future. In 1983 we encounter once again major decisions that will determine the course of our nuclear weapons policy till the end of the century and beyond. These decisions present challenges and opportunities to our citizens, scientists, and government. I have already commented on the MX. I expect there will be a full debate on deterrence and the role of the MX now that the President has accepted the report of the Scowcroft Commission, including the recommendation to deploy one hundred MX missiles in Minuteman silos (see Appendix).

President Reagan has now raised a new issue that goes to the very heart of deterrence and is potentially of greater importance than whether our new strategic forces include MXs, more Trident ships and missiles, and so on. On March 23 the President described to the nation his vision of the future in which we are protected against nuclear weapons by a space-age defense and no longer have to live in a balance of terror. Toward accomplishing this goal of an impenetrable defensive umbrella, he proposed a major new technological initiative. At the same time he acknowledged that it might not be possible to accomplish this goal before the end of the century, and that it may take even longer. He indicated further that our new initiative for defense would be consistent with the strictures of the

74

ABM treaty of SALT I, and he called on scientists to contribute to help him realize his vision.

It is by no means evident to me that what President Reagan is calling for is more than a pipe dream—or the equivalent of asking scientists to build a perpetual motion machine. But the very fact of the President's announcement, and particularly the measures undertaken as a result of it in the years ahead, can have a profound effect on the entire gamut of nuclear policy issues: the arms race, deterrence, stability, and survival. Think for just a moment what the impact would be in this country if Yuri Andropov had made a similar call!

The good news is that this issue is itself not shrouded in secrecy or ignored in the shadows of apathy. To the contrary. In the press, in the churches, in civic organizations, in universities, and in the political arena, a process of education about deterrence has begun in earnest, and nuclear weapons policy is commanding priority attention at this time. There now exists an active and concerned arms control constituency ready to participate in a national debate that we all should welcome—scientists, government, and citizens alike.

Inevitably there are technical details of military technology that must remain secret, but watch out for the argument that goes: "Because of secrecy I can't tell you, but if you knew what I know you would agree with me," etc., etc. This implies that the technical secrets are so important that informed arguments are not possible if one does not have access to these secrets. When arguments have to fall back on this line you can be pretty sure that "the emperor has no clothes." In fact, the issue of new "wonder weapons" goes far beyond any single technical achievement. Many difficult judgments are required about how such complex systems will operate in battle against nuclear bombs, what a determined opponent can do to counter and defeat them, and what their impact on arms control will be.

First let me review some of the issues and problems of the new wonder weapons of space as I see them. At present, both the United States and the Soviet Union are diligently pursuing research on exotic concepts and technologies for space defense—all in accord with the limits in the ABM treaty of SALT I. In particular, article 5 of that treaty specifically states: "Each party undertakes not to develop, test, or deploy ABM systems or components which are sea-based, air-based, space-based, or mobile land-based." That article presents a severe limit on the ability of the Soviet Union and the United States to develop new technologies for ABM. It was negotiated in 1972 precisely with that intention.

In contrast to the ABM situation, which involves research and conceptual ideas only, we are currently developing antisatellite weapons. The Russian approach is to launch missiles from the ground for direct intercept of satellites in low earth orbits up to a few hundred miles above ground. The United States is developing small homing rockets for this purpose which will be launched from F-15 aircraft in flight.

Concepts for the next generation of defensive wonder weapons based in space or on the ground cover a range of more advanced technologies. The most developed of these is a space-based laser system, but other technologies include directed-energy weapons using particle beams as well as X-ray lasers pumped by nuclear explosives. The systems would be designed to attack and destroy all means of delivery of nuclear weapons in order to provide an effective defense: land- and sea-based ballistic missiles shortly after launch when they are most vulnerable, and preferably before they have released their many MIRV warheads, and the air-breathing threat of aircraft and cruise missiles.

In considering these new wonder weapons one needs to analyze the operational problems of a full system utilizing several different technologies, as well as the countermeasures available to an opponent in order to defeat it. I will illustrate the practical problems by considering a space-based laser system alone, since, of all the advanced defense concepts, it is the one for which the technology is best understood. Also for the moment let us consider only the current Soviet ICBM force as presenting a threat—that is, we will ignore their submarine-based ballistic missiles and their air-breathing threat as well as future evolution of the threat in time. The magnitude of the problem is set then by the requirement to destroy all ICBMs launched in a massive attack. If but 5 percent were to get through the defense, some 300 Soviet warheads would arrive at our cities, each warhead being many times larger than the atom bomb that destroyed Hiroshima—anywhere from 30 to 1,000 times larger. Such a defense would hardly provide the escape from a nuclear balance of terror. In order to attack all the ICBMs in a massive launch there would have to be typically some ten laser battle stations in orbit over the ICBM launch area. Multiply this by another factor of twenty in order to provide continuous coverage of the launch areas, since the lasers would necessarily be circling the earth in relatively low orbits in order to deliver enough well-focused energy to burn a hole through the rocket engine. Each of these several hundred battle stations would be very complex and expensive—requiring pointing, aiming, and tracking to accuracies of better than parts per million. Furthermore, their reflecting mirrors will be immense—beyond presently demonstrated structures on the ground—and the lasers will require enormous power. We are therefore talking about several hundred laser stations, each of which, as presently envisaged, would require a fair number of shuttle launches to assemble.

And what would our opponent be doing all the time it takes to assemble such a system? Presumably, not sitting idly by. He may or may not risk disrupting it during its vulnerable assembly phase, but he surely could position antisatellite satellites, or even small space mines, in nearby orbits to activate against it in the event of future conflict. Then one must also consider the vulnerability of the large space-based laser mirror to damage by ground-based directed energy. Many other countermeasures are also available—for example, decoys to divert the laser beam and surface coatings for the missiles similar to that of the laser's mirror to reflect the destructive energy. I have not even added the further requirements against missiles launched from submarines located in widely dispersed regions that would also require constant coverage. And, finally, there is the air-breathing threat—the aircraft and the cruise missiles that can be launched by ships or airplanes from many points around the world and that never rise above the atmosphere to be engaged and destroyed.

These examples illustrate why it so important to avoid the trap called "the fallacy of the last move" when thinking about new wonder weapons and sniffing the sweet appeal of exotic new ABM technologies. The magical new weapon will provoke a response designed to defeat it; and all experience with nuclear weapons has indicated that the advantage lies with the offense, because the destructive power of these weapons is so great that, as I already noted, a defense must be essentially 100 percent perfect or it is useless in defending one's society.

The gap between the President's vision of a future defense and technical realities is enormous. The magnitude of this gap is emphasized by the testimony[*] of Major General Donald Lamberson, head of the Pentagon's directed-energy weapons program, including the space-based laser. He appeared before the Senate Armed Services Committee just hours before the President's call for an intensified effort to build a missile defense and testified that a "constellation of space laser platforms" might be able to stop only half of a large intercontinental missile attack against the United States. By inadvertence the declassified version of 1981 Pentagon testimony before the same Senate committee revealed an estimated cost of $500 billion for such a system aimed at achieving nationwide defense. It would be far less expensive and much simpler for the offense to increase its number of threatening warheads

[*]From a report by Charles Mohr in the *New York Times*, March 31, 1983.

in order to compensate for potential losses to such a defensive system.

Costs aside, I have no idea how to get from here to there with an effective defense. In this judgment I am not alone. In his speech President Reagan called on scientists to help him achieve his vision of escaping out from under the nuclear balance of terror. I share the President's wish that we might remove the threat of nuclear holocaust, and my own long involvement in national security problems has had as its principal aim the goal of reducing, if not removing, that threat. Unfortunately, however, it is not possible to escape the technical realities. Security cannot be mandated, coerced, or simply hoped for. I see no prospect—in space or on the ground, with particle beams or interceptor missiles—of escaping from the present balance of terror. I have not found, nor do I foresee, any technological escape route from the arduous path of serious arms control. It is entirely appropriate—and prudent—for the United States to pursue a research program in advanced and exotic defense concepts, as we are already doing. So are the Russians. It is our hedge against technological surprise. But we should not be misled, nor distracted from today's existing dangers, by technological mirages of a distant future.

One also has to recognize the potentially harmful effects for deterrence of the kind of major effort the President has called for. The undertaking of a major project to construct an exotic space-age defense is very likely to stimulate further buildup of offensive weapons. Quite simply, both the United States and the Soviet Union will further increase their offensive arms to offset whatever partial effectiveness may be achieved by such a system. This is what happened before the SALT I ABM treaty and led to MIRVs. Inevitably, the pattern will be repeated.

In this sense the President's speech itself, with its call for an intensified effort, may prove to have an escalating effect. I am also concerned about the impact of this effort on the SALT I treaty. Since the development of advanced technologies and system concepts for a space-based defense will require actual testing before they can progress very far, there will be pressures to abrogate SALT I and its testing prohibitions on defensive systems. If that happens, our most important arms control achievement to date will have been sacrificed and a questionable technological imperative will have won out over a proven arms control achievement.

We are now approaching a point of no return before the United States and the Soviet Union commit themselves to this new dimension of arms competition in space. Before it is too late to turn back, both countries should consider seriously—and talk to one another—to decide whether or not it is in our mutual interests to go ahead with weapons of war in space. A draft treaty banning all space weapons and attacks against satellites was presented at the United Nations by the Soviet Union more than a year ago. It should be explored further in negotiations. If we have a better idea, let us respond with a proposal of our own. We do, after all, have a very attractive alternative to simply continuing our "monkey-see, monkey-do" pattern of chasing each other and escalating the arms competition with more and more new weapons; and that is to turn to negotiations and cooperative ventures instead of military competition. If President Reagan's vision is so attractive, why not work jointly to achieve it?

I anticipate—and welcome—a national debate on this basic issue of deterrence versus space-age defense. All of us have a vital stake in its outcome. In contrast to the original H-bomb decision, this issue is before the public; and indeed the public is alerted and ready to participate as an active constituency for arms control. Such a constituency is the ingredient we needed and lacked at the time of the MIRV decision and the debate in the Senate over SALT II ratification.

CONCLUSION

Although the President failed to convince me of the practical reality of his space wars vision, his speech did convince me that effective use is not being made of scientific input in technical defense issues at the highest level. I was reminded of the lament by former British Prime Minister Harold Macmillan about the gap between the realities of science and government leaders. In his book *Pointing the Way* (London: Macmillan, 1972) Macmillan wrote: "In all these affairs Prime Ministers, Ministers of Defence and Cabinets are under a great handicap. The technicalities and uncertainties of the sophisticated weapons which they have to authorize are out of the range of normal experience. There is today a far greater gap between their own knowledge and the expert advice which they receive than there has ever been in the history of war."

This gap must be closed. The government cannot

dispense with the scientist. It has an obligation to arrange for the best possible scientific analysis and advice before making its decisions or raising false expectations, as in this example of "star wars" which now threatens to be a highly politicized issue. Furthermore, the scientific advice must be neutral and free of political and doctrinal biases. This is not easy to achieve. Scientists may be experts, but they are also human. Hard as we try to avoid it, personal biases do occasionally cloud, if not merely fog, our professional judgment—although some of us manage to control our biases better than others. Therefore, a diverse body of experts is needed to provide balanced, as well as informed, judgments. This, of course, is precisely the problem C. P. Snow described in his Godkin Lectures. He used the example of two British scientists, Sir Henry Tizard and F. A. Lindemann, who were antagonists in the pre–World War II debate over radar, to convey his concern that balanced judgments must be presented.

President Eisenhower understood these issues well when he created, in 1958, the position of a full-time science adviser in the White House and also established the President's Science Advisory Committee, which served the President and the nation well for more than a decade before it was disbanded in 1974. He also showed his wisdom when he responded to a question about the political affiliation of his scientific advisers with the reported comment: "I don't want to know." (Comments like that can almost make one nostalgic for the past.)

Like the government, scientists as a community also

face an obligation to provide the best advice—some through public channels and some through the advisory process as each individual sees fit. We need both. Those who follow the route of Oppenheimer and Sakharov—no matter how small their niche—may and, as I well know, often do suffer disillusionment similar to theirs.

Although scientists may bring important physical insights to an understanding of the enormity of the catastrophe of a nuclear war, the problem of working to avoid one is not ours alone. Ultimately, mankind has to recognize that we have no choice but to reject war entirely. In Henry IV, Part II (4.1.67-69), Shakespeare has the Archbishop of York justify his path of insurrection to the Earl of Westmoreland with these words:

> I have in equal balance justly weigh'd
> What wrongs our arms may do,
>   what wrongs we suffer,
> And find our griefs heavier than our offences.

But that was before nuclear weapons so changed the nature of war. Since Hiroshima the inescapable and difficult question of our time has been the one posed by Father Siemes, a Jesuit priest writing to the Holy See in Rome from the rubble of Hiroshima: "The crux of the matter is whether total war in its present form is justifiable, even when it serves a just purpose."

However difficult the path in our slow evolutionary voyage, we must catch up with the nuclear revolution—and the sooner the safer. As we navigate the treacherous seas of nuclear deterrence the distant goal of world without war can serve as our beacon, like the distant star of Robert Frost, "to stay our minds on and be staid."

Appendix

Comments on the Scowcroft Report and the MX

The Scowcroft Report covers a broad range of issues of arms control and strategic nuclear force modernization. In making its recommendations the report emphasizes the importance of creating a political consensus and of achieving continuity of policy and bipartisan support for the programs it advocates. It cuts important ground with its analysis leading to these three conclusions with which I fully concur:

1. The theoretical vulnerability of the U.S. Minuteman force of land-based ICBMs should be viewed in the context of overall force structure. The report does this and recognizes practical problems faced by the attacker, especially the problem of attack timing that makes it impossible for the Soviets simultaneously to mount a threatening attack against both the ICBMs and the alert bomber force of the United States. As a result, the report gently closes the "window of vulnerability" which has been prominent in recent political rhetoric.

2. In future arms control negotiations the aggregate number of warheads should be limited in the counting rules. This is a change from the past, in

which launchers were counted. The importance and virtues of a warhead-counting approach are a central part of the discussion in my second chapter. I also welcome the emphasis in the report on arms control as an important part of our national security considerations and decisions.

3. Stability should be a primary objective of our efforts in arms control and in modernizing our forces. In order to improve stability we should start developing strategic weapons whose *individual* value and importance are reduced. In particular, engineering development of a small single-warhead ICBM, with initial operational capability in the early 1990s, is recommended as a step toward a more secure land-based deterrent and thereby improved crisis stability. Similarly, a small submarine is endorsed as a follow-on to the large Trident submarine, which is of very high military value.

My major differences with the Scowcroft Report—and they are serious differences—concern its discussion of the fundamentals of deterrence and its recommendation that the United States deploy 100 MX missiles in vulnerable Minuteman silos. This discussion is summarized in the sentence "deployment of MX is essential in order to remove the Soviet advantage in ICBM capability and to help deter the threat of conventional or limited nuclear attacks on the alliance." This is a call for nuclear war-fighting. That is, a prompt counterforce capability against hardened military targets, including missile silos and command posts, is stated as a requirement to deter conventional attack. This call is directly counter to the arguments for deterrence, including flexible response, that I presented in the first chapter; and I reject it for the reasons given there.

The report emphasizes, "Effective deterrence of any Soviet temptation to threaten or launch a massive conventional or a limited nuclear war thus requires us to have a comparable ability to destroy Soviet military targets, hardened and otherwise. . . . A one-sided strategic condition in which the Soviet Union could effectively destroy the whole range of strategic targets in the United States, but we could not effectively destroy a similar range of targets in the Soviet Union, would be extremely unstable over the long run." What this statement ignores is the very strong diversity of the U.S. strategic deterrent which loads less than one-fourth of our warheads on the ICBMs in fixed, hardened, and now potentially (theoretically) vulnerable silos. In contrast, the Soviets have some three-fourths of their force so deployed. Therefore, a massive threat to that force will be destablizing, not stabilizing. The report recognizes this problem in a later paragraph when it argues that the recommended deployment of "on the order of 100 MX missiles in existing Minuteman silos" would not threaten stability because there would not be a "sufficient number of warheads to be able to attack all hardened Soviet ICBMs, much less all of the many command posts and other hardened military targets in the Soviet Union." I agree with the concern expressed in the report. But once we add 1,000 warheads on 100 MX missiles to the 300 Minutemen III missiles that have already been upgraded and are capable of delivering 900 very accurate warheads and we further deploy the (also) recommended very accurate Trident II missile, the threat may understandably seem much more ominous to the Russians—and thereby a cause for further escalation. In particular, warheads designed for hard-target counterforce and deployed in vulnerable silos are antithetical to deterrence. Their characteristics are appropriate for first strike only. Stuffing the MX into Minuteman silos will *increase* the vulnerability of U.S. forces, for, as Senator John Tower said on November 2, 1981: "we're creating just so many more sitting ducks for the Russians to shoot at." Since the MX is so powerful and threatening as a first-strike weapon and is, therefore, so valuable as a target, this will surely add to crisis *instability*. It will add pressure toward a policy of "launch on warning" or "launch under attack," requiring a highly automated, hair-trigger command and control chain. I therefore find great potential danger in creating a *vulnerable* and sizable prompt hard-target kill capability.

The most intriguing argument for the MX in the report is the allegation that it is needed to demonstrate "our national will and cohesion" and that "abandoning the MX at this time in search of a substitute would jeopardize, not enhance, the likelihood of reaching a stabilizing and equitable agreement" with the Soviets. That is nothing more or less than an exercise in psychology and an unprovable political assertion. I find it unconvincing, as I also do the assumption in the report that we got the ABM treaty of 1972 in SALT I only because we made a decision to start deploying our own ABM system.

As to national will, the United States has already made a very substantial commitment to a major strategic modernization program—including Trident ships and missiles, several kinds of bombers and cruise missiles, plus in all probability the small single-warhead ICBM proposed in the report. I find that very strong evidence of a will and willingness to spend for national defense! Isn't it time to give intelligent choices and a small measure of restraint some priority over more and more weapons?

Aside from my differences with the Scowcroft Report on the meaning of deterrence and the desirability, much less the need, for "on the order of 100 missiles," I highly commend this report for carrying the debate to issues well beyond the MX and its basing mode. I agree with its technical judgments. I am also thankful to the report for rejecting previously proposed MX basing schemes, such as Densepack, Racetrack, etc., and for closing the "window of vulnerability." But I fail to see the logic in its recommendation to deploy the MX. On this score the report is every inch a political document, expressing the political consensus of a bipartisan group of very senior analysts of national security, almost all of whom in the past have advocated the MX.

What will be of interest and considerable national importance is how the newly created public arms control constituency will respond to this "establishment" political consensus. Following the President's acceptance of the recommendations in this report, Congress has to act on his request for funds for continuing the MX project through engineering studies into construction. On successive days, May 24 and 25, 1983, the House and Senate voted to release fiscal year 1983 funds to continue engineering development and tests of the MX. Congress has yet to authorize and to appropriate fiscal year 1984 funds to initiate procurement of the missile. I hope that there will be a substantive debate—particularly about the meaning of deterrence—and that the public will make its views known. The final disposition of the MX will probably become clear only after several years and extended discussion. I also expect that arms control actions and attitudes of the Soviet Union will figure prominently in the eventual fate of the MX missile.

The Danger of Thermonuclear War:

AN OPEN LETTER TO DR. SIDNEY DRELL

Andrei Sakharov

Dear Friend:

I have read your two splendid lectures—the speech on nuclear weapons at Grace Cathedral, October 23, 1982, and the opening statement to Hearings on the Consequences of Nuclear War before the Subcommit-

---

Reprinted by permission from *Foreign Affairs* (summer 1983). The Editor of *Foreign Affairs* is grateful to Professor Drell and to Strobe Talbott for their help in refining the translation of technical terms, and in preparing the explanatory Editor's Notes, for which of course the Editor takes responsibility.

Dr. Drell's speech at Grace Cathedral (in San Francisco) is unpublished but available from him on request. His opening statement before the Subcommittee on Investigations and Oversight of the House Committee on Science and Technology is contained in the Committee's record of those hearings, *The Consequences of Nuclear War on the Global Environment*, September 15, 1982, p. 6.

tee on Investigations and Oversight. What you say and write about the appalling dangers of nuclear war is very close to my heart and has disturbed me profoundly for many years now. I decided to address an open letter to you, feeling it necessary to take part in the discussion of this problem, one of the most important facing mankind.

In full agreement with your general theses, I will express certain considerations of a more specific nature which, I think, need to be taken into account when making decisions. These considerations in part contradict some of your statements and in part supplement and, possibly, amplify them. It seems to me that my opinion communicated here in open discussion can prove of interest in view of my scientific, technological, and psychological experience, acquired in the period when I took part in work on thermonuclear weapons, and also because I am one of the few independent participants in this discussion in the U.S.S.R.

II

I fully agree with your assessment of the danger of nuclear war. In view of the critical importance of this thesis, I will dwell on it in some detail, perhaps repeating what is already well known.

Here, and later on, I use the terms "nuclear war" and "thermonuclear war" nearly interchangeably. Nuclear weapons mean atomic and thermonuclear weapons: conventional weapons mean any weapons with the exception of three types with the capability of mass destruction—nuclear, chemical, and bacteriological weapons.

A large nuclear war would be a calamity of indescribable proportions and absolutely unpredictable consequences, with the uncertainties tending toward the worse.

According to data from United Nations experts, by the end of 1980 the world's overall supply of nuclear weapons consisted of 50,000 nuclear charges.* The total power of these charges (most of which are in the 0.04- to 20-megaton range) amounts to 13,000 megatons according to the experts' estimates. The figures you have presented are not in conflict with those estimates. In this regard you mention that the total power of all the explosives used in the Second World War did not exceed six megatons (three megatons, according to the estimates with which I am familiar). However, when making this comparison one must take into account the greater relative efficacy of smaller charges with the same total power, but that does not alter the qualitative conclusions about the colossal destructive power of the nuclear weapons that have been amassed.

You also cite data according to which the U.S.S.R. at the present time (1982) has 8,000 thermonuclear charges deployed and the United States 9,000.**

---

* *Editor's Note*. "Charge" is a standard Soviet term—used frequently in arms control negotiations—embracing warheads on ballistic missiles and also armaments aboard bombers, which may be in bomb or missile form. There is a separate Russian word for warheads.

** *Editor's Note*. These totals refer to the number of charges deployed on intercontinental ballistic missiles, submarine-launched ballistic missiles, and intercontinental-range bombers.

Many of these charges are warheads on ballistic missiles, and many of these are multiple independently-targetable reentry vehicles (MIRVs). It should be noted that the basis of the U.S.S.R.'s arsenal (70 percent, according to statements by TASS) consists of gigantic land-based missiles (in silos) and somewhat smaller intermediate-range missiles, on mobile launchers. Eighty percent of the U.S. arsenal consists of submarine-based nuclear missiles, much smaller but less vulnerable than silo-based missiles, and also of strategic bombers carrying nuclear bombs, some of which are apparently very powerful. It is doubtful whether masses of aircraft could penetrate Soviet territory deeply—but a more precise assessment of their capabilities must take the possibilities of cruise missiles into account; these would probably be able to penetrate the enemy's air defense systems.

Currently, the most powerful American ICBMs (I am not speaking of the planned MX) possess several times less throw-weight than the principal land-based Soviet missiles.* The American ones carry fewer MIRVs, and the yield of their warheads is less. (It is assumed that when dividing the throw-weight of a missile among several warheads—let's say ten—the aggregate yield of the multiple warheads is less than

* *Editor's Note.* The term "throw-weight" is normally defined as the weight of effective payload that can be delivered to an intended distance; effective payload may include penetration aids and navigational equipment as well as the nuclear charge itself. The term "yield" refers to destructive power, and the term "compact targets," as used in this paragraph, clearly refers to military targets in general and to specially hardened ICBM sites in particular.

the yield of a large single warhead on the same missile. But MIRVs greatly increase the ability of one side to attack compact targets on the other. MIRVs are also highly destructive against targets spread out over a wide area such as large cities. The aggregate yield may be less than that of a large single warhead, but the destructiveness will remain high because of the multiple blasts spread out over the area. I have dwelt on these details since they may prove of substance in further discussion.)

You cite the estimates of the international journal of the Royal Swedish Academy, according to which an attack on the principal cities of the Northern Hemisphere by 5,000 warheads with a total power of 2,000 megatons will kill 750 million people as a result of the shock wave alone.*

I would like to add the following to that estimate:

1. The overall number of long-range nuclear weapons possessed by the five nuclear powers is three or four times greater than the figure used in the Swedish estimate and their overall power is six to seven times greater. The accepted average number of casualties per missile—250,000 people—cannot be considered an overestimate if one compares the accepted average power of a thermonuclear charge of 400 kilotons with the power of the 17-kiloton explosion at Hiroshima and the number of victims from its shock waves, no fewer than 40,000.

2. An extremely important factor in the destruc-

---

* *Editor's Note.* This estimate is contained in the publication of the Royal Swedish Academy, *Ambio,* Vol. XI, Nos. 2–3, 1982.

tive capability of nuclear weapons is thermal radiation. The fires at Hiroshima were the cause of a significant portion (up to 50 percent) of the fatalities. With the increase of the charges' power, the relative role of thermal radiation increases. Therefore, this factor significantly increases the number of direct casualties.

3. During an attack on especially dense, compact enemy targets (like silo-based missile launchers, command points, communication centers, government institutions, shelters, and other of the more important targets) it must be assumed that a significant portion of the explosions will be ground-level or low. In such cases there inevitably will be "traces," bands of dust fallout raised by the explosion from the surface and "impregnated" by the products of uranium fission. Therefore, although the direct radioactive effect of a nuclear charge takes place in a zone where everything alive is, in any case, annihilated by the shock wave and by fire, its indirect effect—through fallout—proves very substantial. The area contaminated by fallout so that the total dose of radiation exceeds the safety limit of 300 roentgens is, for a typical one-megaton nuclear charge, thousands of square kilometers!

During the ground-level test of the Soviet thermonuclear charge in August 1953, tens of thousands of people were evacuated beforehand from the zone where fallout was possible. People were only able to return to the settlement of Kara-aul in the spring of 1954! In war conditions an orderly evacuation is impossible. Hundreds of millions will flee in panic, often from one contaminated zone into another. Hundreds of millions of people will inevitably become the victims of radioactive irradiation, the mass migrations of people will make the chaos, the deterioration of sanitary conditions and the hunger all the greater. The genetic consequences of irradiation will threaten man as a biological species and all animal and plant life on the Earth.

I entirely agree with your basic idea that mankind has *never* encountered anything even remotely resembling a large nuclear war in scale and horror.

No matter how appalling the direct consequences of nuclear explosions, we cannot exclude that the indirect effects will be even more substantial. The indirect effects could be fatal for modern society, which is extraordinarily complex and thus highly vulnerable.

The general ecological consequences are just as dangerous, although by virtue of the complex nature of ecological interdependencies, forecasts and estimates are extremely difficult here. I will mention some of the problems discussed in the literature (in your talks, in particular) without assessing their seriousness, although I am certain that many of the dangers indicated are entirely real:

1. Continuous forest fires could destroy the greater part of the planet's forests. The smoke involved would destroy the transparency of the atmosphere. A night lasting many weeks would ensue on Earth followed by a lack of oxygen in the atmosphere. As a result, this factor alone, if real, could destroy life on the planet. In less pronounced form, this factor could have important ecological, economic, and psychological consequences.

2. High-altitude wartime nuclear explosions in space (particularly the thermonuclear explosion of ABM missiles and the explosion of attacking missiles whose purpose is to disrupt enemy radar) could possibly destroy or seriously damage the ozone layer pro-

tecting Earth from the sun's ultraviolet radiation. Estimates of this danger are very imprecise—if the maximal estimates are true then this factor is sufficient to destroy life.

3. Disruption of transportation and communication could prove critical in the complex modern world.

4. No doubt there will be a (complete or partial) disruption in the production and distribution of food, in water supply and sewage, in fuel and electric service, and in medicine and clothing—all on a continent-wide scale. The public health-care system will be disrupted, sanitary conditions will revert to a medieval level and may become even worse than that. It will be impossible in practice to provide medical assistance to the hundreds of millions who have been wounded, burned, or exposed to radiation.

5. Hunger and epidemics in a context of chaos and devastation could take more lives than the nuclear explosions would take directly. It is also not out of the question that, along with the "ordinary" diseases which will inevitably spread far and wide—influenza, cholera, dysentery, typhus, anthrax, plague, and others—entirely new diseases could arise as the result of the radiation-caused mutation of viruses as well as especially dangerous forms of the old diseases against which people and animals would have no immunity.

6. It is especially difficult to foresee mankind's maintaining any social stability in conditions of universal chaos. Great gangs will kill and terrorize people and struggle among themselves in keeping with the laws of the criminal world: "You die today, I'll die tomorrow."

Of course, our experience of social upheaval and war

demonstrates that mankind possesses unexpected reserves; people's vitality in extreme situations surpasses what could have been imagined a priori. But even if mankind were able to preserve itself as a social body, which seems highly unlikely, the most important social institutions—the foundation of civilization—would be destroyed.

In sum, it should be said that all-out nuclear war would mean the destruction of contemporary civilization, hurl man back centuries, cause the deaths of hundreds of millions or billions of people, and, with a certain degree of probability, would cause the annihilation of life on earth.

Clearly it is meaningless to speak of victory in a large nuclear war which is collective suicide.

I think that basically my point of view coincides with yours as well as with the opinion of a great many people on earth.

III

I am also in complete agreement with your other conclusions. I agree that if the "nuclear threshold" is crossed, i.e., if any country uses a nuclear weapon even on a limited scale, the further course of events would be difficult to control and the most probable result would be swift escalation leading from a nuclear war initially limited in scale or by region to an all-out nuclear war, i.e., to general suicide.

It is relatively unimportant how the "nuclear threshold" is crossed—as a result of a preventive nuclear strike or in the course of a war fought with conventional weapons, when a country is threatened with defeat, or simply as a result of an accident (technical or organizational).

In view of the above, I am convinced that the following basic tenet of yours is true: *Nuclear weapons only make sense as a means of deterring nuclear aggression by a potential enemy,* i.e., a nuclear war cannot be planned with the aim of winning it. Nuclear weapons cannot be viewed as a means of restraining aggressions carried out by means of conventional weapons.

Of course you realize that this last statement is in contradiction to the West's actual strategy in the last few decades. For a long time, beginning as far back as the end of the 1940s, the West has not been relying on its "conventional" armed forces as a means sufficient for repelling a potential aggressor and for restraining expansions. There are many reasons for this—the West's lack of political, military, and economic unity; the striving to avoid a peacetime militarization of the economy, society, technology, and science; the low numerical levels of the Western nations' armies. All that at a time when the U.S.S.R. and the other countries of the socialist camp have armies with great numerical strength and are rearming them intensively, sparing no resources. It is possible that for a limited period of time the mutual nuclear terror had a certain restraining effect on the course of world events. But, at the present time, the balance of nuclear terror is a dangerous remnant of the past! In order to avoid aggression with conventional weapons one cannot threaten to use nuclear weapons if their use is inadmissible. One of the conclusions that follows here—and a conclusion you draw—is that it is necessary to restore strategic parity in the field of conventional weapons. This you expressed somewhat differently, and without stressing the point.

Meanwhile this is a very important and non-trivial statement which must be dwelt on in some detail.

The restoration of strategic parity is only possible by investing large resources and by an essential change in the psychological atmosphere in the West. There must be a readiness to make certain limited economic sacrifices and, most important, an understanding of the seriousness of the situation and of the necessity for some restructuring. In the final analysis, this is necessary to prevent nuclear war, and war in general. Will the West's politicians be able to carry out such a restructuring? Will the press, the public, and our fellow scientists help them (and not hinder them as is frequently now the case)? Can they succeed in convincing those who doubt the necessity of such restructuring? A great deal depends on it—the opportunity for the West to conduct a nuclear arms policy that will be conducive to the lessening of the danger of nuclear disaster.

In any case, I am very glad that you (and earlier, in another context, Professor Panofsky) have spoken out in favor of strategic parity in the area of conventional weapons.*

In conclusion, I should stress especially that restructuring of strategy could of course only be carried out gradually and very carefully in order to prevent a loss of parity in some of the intermediate phases.

* *Editor's Note.* The reference here is to Wolfgang K. H. Panofsky, Professor of Physics at Stanford and Director of the Stanford Linear Accelerator Center. Professor Panofsky notes that the statement accurately reflects his views.

IV

As I have understood them, your further thoughts on nuclear weapons per se amount to the following:

It is necessary to conduct a balanced reduction of the nuclear arsenal, and a first stage in this process of nuclear disarmament might be a mutual freeze on the currently existing nuclear arsenals. I will quote you: "Decisions in the area of nuclear weapons should be based simply on the criterion of achieving a reliable deterrent and not on other additional demands relating to nuclear war since, generally speaking, such demands are not limited by anything and are not realistic." This is one of your central theses.

For talks on nuclear disarmament you propose that one quite simple—and, within the limits of the possible, fair—criterion for assessing nuclear strength be worked out. As that criterion you propose taking the sum total of the number of delivery vehicles and the total number of nuclear charges which can be delivered (probably one should assume the maximal number of certain standard or conventional charges which can be delivered by a given type of missile with a corresponding division of the usable weight).

I will begin by discussing that latter proposal of yours (made jointly with your student, Kent Wisner). * This proposal seems practical to me. Your crite-

* *Editor's Note.* The proposal was originally set forth in Sidney D. Drell and Kent F. Wisner, "A New Formula for Nuclear Arms Control," *International Security,* Winter 1980/81, pp. 186–194, and is refined in Dr. Drell's "L + RV: A Formula for Arms Control," *The Bulletin of the Atomic Scientists,* April 1982, pp. 28–34.

rion takes into account delivery vehicles of various throw-weights by assigning them various weight factors. This is very important—the assigning of an equal weight factor to both the small American missiles and the large Soviet missiles was one of the points for which I, at one time, criticized the SALT I Treaty (while in general viewing the very fact of the talks and the concluding of the Treaty in a positive light). Here, in distinction to criteria using the power of the charge, as a rule not published officially, the number of deliverable charges is easy to determine. Your criterion also takes into account the fact that, for example, five missiles each carrying one warhead have a significant tactical advantage over one large missile carrying five warheads. Of course, the criterion you propose does not encompass all the parameters like distance, accuracy, or degree of vulnerability—they will have to be allowed for supplementarily or, in some cases, not taken into account so as to facilitate agreements.

I hope that your (or some analogous) criterion will be accepted as the basis for negotiations both on intercontinental missiles and (independently) on medium-range missiles. In both cases it will be much more difficult than it now is to insist on unfair conditions in the agreements and possible to move from word to deed more swiftly. Most likely, the very acceptance of your (or an analogous) criterion will require a diplomatic and propaganda struggle—but it's worth it.

V

From this relatively specific question I will move to one more general, more complex and controversial. Is it actually possible when making decisions in the area of nuclear weapons to ignore all the considerations and requirements relevant to the possible scenarios for a nuclear war and simply limit oneself to the criterion of achieving a reliable deterrent—when that criterion is understood to mean an arsenal sufficient to deal a devastating blow in response? Your answer to this question—while perhaps formulating it somewhat differently—is positive and you draw far-reaching conclusions.

There is no doubt that at present the United States already possesses a large number of submarine-based missiles and charges carried by strategic bombers which are not vulnerable to the U.S.S.R. and, in addition, has silo-based missiles though they are smaller than the U.S.S.R.'s—all these in such amounts that, were those charges used against the U.S.S.R., nothing, roughly speaking, would be left of it. You maintain that this has *already* created a reliable deterrent—independently of what the U.S.S.R. and the United States have and what they lack! Therefore, you specifically consider the building of the MX missile unnecessary and similarly consider irrelevant the arguments which are advanced in support of developing it—the U.S.S.R.'s substantial arsenal of intercontinental missiles with large throw-weight which the United States does not have; and the fact that Soviet missiles and MX missiles have multiple warheads so that one missile can destroy several enemy silos during a missile duel. Therefore you consider it acceptable (with certain reservations) for the United States to freeze the nuclear arsenals of the United States and the U.S.S.R. at their current numerical levels.*

Your line of reasoning seems to me very strong and convincing. But I think that the concept presented fails to take into account all the complex realities of the opposition that involves two world systems and that there is the necessity (despite your stance) for a more specific and comprehensive unbiased consideration than a simple orientation toward a "reliable deterrent" (in the meaning of the word as formulated above, i.e., the possibility of dealing a devastating retaliatory strike). I will endeavor to explain this statement.

Precisely because an all-out nuclear war means collective suicide, we can imagine that a potential aggressor might count on a lack of resolve on the part of the country under attack to take the step leading to that suicide, i.e., it could count on its victim capitulating for the sake of saving what could be saved. Given that, if the aggressor has a military advantage in some of the variants of conventional warfare or—which is also possible *in principle*—in some of the variants of partial (limited) nuclear war, he would attempt to use the fear

---

* *Editor's Note.* Professor Drell notes that maintaining the U.S. and Soviet nuclear arsenals at their present numerical levels is not the same as the kind of "freeze" usually discussed today—in that it would not preclude changes in the types of weapons within the numerical level. As to a strict "freeze" as usually discussed, Professor Drell's position, stated in his Grace Cathedral speech, is that "the freeze movement has been very helpful in creating . . . a constituency for arms control. Though I recognize some deficiencies of the freeze as literal policy, I support it and will vote for it as a mandate for arms control . . . ."

of further escalation to force the enemy to fight the war on his (the aggressor's) own terms. There would be little cause for joy if, ultimately, the aggressor's hopes proved false and the aggressor country perished along with the rest of mankind.

You consider it necessary to achieve a restoration of strategic parity in the field of conventional arms. Now take the next logical step—while nuclear weapons exist it is also necessary to have strategic parity in relation to those variants of limited or regional nuclear warfare which a potential enemy could impose, i.e., it is really *necessary* to examine in detail the various scenarios for both conventional and nuclear war and to analyze the various contingencies. It is of course not possible to analyze fully all these possibilities or to ensure security entirely. But I am attempting to warn of the opposite extreme—"closing one's eyes" and relying on one's potential enemy to be perfectly sensible. As always in life's complex problems, some sort of compromise is needed.

Of course I realize that in attempting not to lag behind a potential enemy in any way, we condemn ourselves to an arms race that is tragic in a world with so many critical problems admitting of no delay. But the main danger is slipping into an all-out nuclear war. *If* the probability of such an outcome could be reduced at the cost of another ten or fifteen years of the arms race, then perhaps that price must be paid while, at the same time, diplomatic, economic, ideological, political, cultural, and social efforts are made to prevent a war.

Of course it would be wiser to agree now to reduce nuclear and conventional weapons and to eliminate nuclear weapons entirely. But is that now possible in a world poisoned with fear and mistrust, a world where the West fears aggression from the U.S.S.R., the U.S.S.R. fears aggression from the West and from China, and where China fears it from the U.S.S.R., and no verbal assurances and treaties can eliminate those dangers entirely?

I know that pacifist sentiments are very strong in the West. I deeply sympathize with people's yearning for peace, for a solution to world problems by peaceful means; I share those aspirations fully. But, at the same time, I am certain that it is absolutely necessary to be mindful of the specific political, military, and strategic realities of the present day and to do so objectively without making any sort of allowances for either side; this also means that one should not proceed from an a priori assumption of any special peace-loving nature in the socialist countries due to their supposed progressiveness or the horrors and losses they have experienced in war. Objective reality is much more complicated and far from anything so simple. People both in the socialist and the Western countries have a passionate inward aspiration for peace. This is an extremely important factor, but, I repeat, itself alone does not exclude the possibility of a tragic outcome.

VI

What is necessary now, I believe, is the enormous practical task of education so that specific, exact, and historically and politically meaningful objective information can be made available to all people, information that will enjoy their trust and not be veiled with dogma and propaganda. Here one must take into account that, in the countries of the West, pro-Soviet propaganda has been conducted for quite a long time and is very goal-oriented and clever, and that pro-Soviet elements have penetrated many key positions, particularly in the mass media.

The history of the pacifist campaigns against the deployment of missiles in Europe is telling in many respects. After all, many of those participating in those campaigns entirely ignore the initial cause of NATO's "dual decision"—the change in strategic parity in the 1970s in favor of the U.S.S.R.—and, when protesting NATO's plans, they have not advanced any demands on the U.S.S.R. Another example: President Carter's attempt to take a minimal step toward achieving balance in the area of conventional arms, i.e., to introduce draft registration, met with stiff resistance. Meanwhile, balance in the area of conventional arms is a necessary prerequisite for reducing nuclear arsenals. For public opinion in the West to assess global problems correctly, in particular the problems of strategic parity both in conventional and in nuclear weapons, a more objective approach, one which takes the real world strategic situation into account, is vitally needed.

VII

A second group of problems in the field of nuclear weapons about which I should make a few supplementary remarks here concerns the talks on nuclear disarmament. For these talks to be successful the West should have something that it can give up! The case of the "Euromissiles" once again demonstrates how difficult it is to negotiate from a position of weakness. Only very recently has the U.S.S.R. apparently ceased to insist on its unsubstantiated thesis that a rough nuclear parity now exists and therefore everything should be left as it is.

Now, the next welcome step would be the reduction of the number of missiles—which must include a fair assessment of the *quality* of missiles and other means of delivery (i.e., the number of charges deliverable by each carrier, its range and accuracy, and its degree of vulnerability—the last being greater for aircraft and less for missiles;* most likely, it would be expedient to use your criterion, or analogous ones). And what is absolutely at issue here is not moving the missiles beyond the Urals but *destroying* them. After all, rebasing is too "reversible." Of course, one also must not consider powerful Soviet missiles, with mobile launchers and several warheads, as being equal to the now-existing Pershing I, the British and French missiles, or the bombs on shot-range bombers—as the Soviet side sometimes attempts to do for purposes of propaganda.

No less important a problem is that of the powerful silo-based missiles. At present the U.S.S.R. has a great advantage in this area. Perhaps talks about the limitation and reduction of these most destructive missiles could become easier if the United States were to have MX missiles, albeit only potentially (indeed, that would be best of all).

---

* *Editor's Note.* The reference to greater relative vulnerability of aircraft vis-à-vis missiles apparently refers to vulnerability to defensive measures in the execution of a mission.

A few words about the military capabilities of powerful missiles: they can be used to deliver the largest thermonuclear charges for destroying cities and other major enemy targets—while for exhausting the enemy's ABM systems there will most likely be a simultaneous use of a "rain" of smaller missiles, false targets and so on. (Much is written about the possibility of developing ABM systems using super-powerful lasers, accelerated particle beams, and so forth. But the creation of an effective defense against missiles along these lines seems highly doubtful to me.) We present the following estimates to give an idea of what a powerful missile attack on a city would be like. Assuming that the maximal power of an individual charge carried by a large rocket would be of a magnitude of 15-25 megatons, we find that the area of complete destruction of dwellings would be 250-400 square kilometers, the area affected by thermal radiation would be 300-500 square kilometers, the zone of radioactive traces (in case of a ground-level explosion) would be 500-1000 kilometers long and 50-100 kilometers wide!

Of equal importance is the fact that powerful MIRVed missiles could be used to destroy compact enemy targets, in particular, similar silo-based enemy missiles. Here is a rough estimate of an attack of that type on launch sites. One hundred MX missiles (the number proposed by the Reagan Administration for the first round of deployment) could carry one thousand 600-kiloton warheads.

Considering the ellipse of concentration* and the

* *Editor's Note.* This phrase is a literal translation from the Russian. It apparently refers to the shape and size of the area in

hardness assumed for the Soviet launch sites, each of the warheads has, according to the data published in the American press, a 60-percent probability of destroying one launch site. During an attack on 500 Soviet launch sites, with two warheads targeted for each site, 16 percent will remain undamaged, i.e., "only" 80 missiles.

A specific danger associated with silo-based missiles is that they can be destroyed relatively easily as a result of enemy attack, as I have just demonstrated. At the same time, they can be used to destroy enemy launch sites in an amount four to five times larger than the number of missiles used for the attack. A country with large numbers of silo-based missiles (at the present time this is primarily the U.S.S.R., but if the United States carries out a major MX program, then it too) could be "tempted" to use such missiles first before the enemy destroys them. In such circumstances the presence of silo-based missiles constitutes a destabilizing factor.

In view of the above, it seems very important to me to strive for the abolition of powerful silo-based missiles at the talks on nuclear disarmament. While the U.S.S.R. is the leader in this field there is very little chance of its easily relinquishing that lead. If it is necessary to spend a few billion dollars on MX missiles to alter this situation, then perhaps this is what the West

---

which a given missile is likely to land in accordance with its accuracy characteristics. The comparable American term is "circular error probable," or "CEP," defined as the area within which a given missile has a 50-percent chance of landing. Such an area is in fact usually elliptical in shape rather than circular.

must do. But, at the same time, if the Soviets, in deed and not just in word, take significant verifiable measures for reducing the number of land-based missiles (more precisely, for destroying them), then the West should not only abolish MX missiles (or not build them!) but carry out other significant disarmament programs as well.

On the whole I am convinced that nuclear disarmament talks are of enormous importance and of the highest priority. They must be conducted continuously—in the brighter periods of international relations but also in the periods when relations are strained—and conducted with persistence, foresight, firmness and, at the same time, with flexibility and initiative. In so doing, political figures should not think of exploiting those talks, and the nuclear problem in general, for their own immediate political gains but only for the long-term interests of their country and the world. And the planning of the talks should be included in one's general nuclear strategy as its most important part—on this point as well I am in agreement with you!

VIII

The third group of problems which should be discussed here is political and social in nature. A nuclear war could result from a conventional war, while a conventional war is, as is well known, a result of politics. We all know that the world is not at peace. There are a variety of reasons for this—national, economic, and social reasons, as well as the tyranny of dictators.

Many of the tragic events now occurring have their

roots in the distant past. It would absolutely be wrong to see only Moscow's hand everywhere. Still, when examining the general trend of events since 1945 there has been a relentless expansion of the Soviet sphere of influence—objectively, this is nothing but Soviet expansion on a world scale. This process has spread as the U.S.S.R. has grown stronger economically (though that strength is one-sided), and in scientific, technological and military terms, and has today assumed proportions dangerously harmful to international equilibrium. The West has grounds to worry that the world's sea routes, Arab oil, and the uranium, diamonds, and other resources of South Africa are now threatened.

One of the basic problems of this age is the fate of the developing countries, the greater part of mankind. But, in fact, for the U.S.S.R., and to some degree for the West as well, this problem has become exploitable and expendable in the struggle for dominance and strategic interests. Millions of people are dying of hunger every year, hundreds of millions suffer from malnutrition and hopeless poverty. The West provides the developing countries with economic and technological aid, but this remains entirely insufficient due largely to the rising price of crude oil. Aid from the U.S.S.R. and the socialist countries is smaller in scale and, to a greater degree than the West's aid, military in nature and bloc-oriented. And, very importantly, that aid is in no way coordinated with world efforts.

The hot spots of local conflicts are not dying but are rather threatening to grow into global wars. All this is greatly alarming.

The most acutely negative manifestation of Soviet policies was the invasion of Afghanistan which began in December 1979 with the murder of the head of state. Three years of appallingly cruel anti-guerrilla war have brought incalculable suffering to the Afghan people, as attested by the more than four million refugees in Pakistan and Iran.

It was precisely the general upsetting of world equilibrium caused by the invasion of Afghanistan and by other concurrent events which was the fundamental reason that the SALT II agreement was not ratified. I am with you in regretting this but I cannot disregard the reasons I have just described.

Yet another subject closely connected to the problem of peace is the openness of society and human rights. I use the term the "openness of society" to mean precisely what the great Niels Bohr meant by it when introducing it more than 30 years ago.

In 1948, the U.N.'s member states adopted the Universal Declaration of Human Rights and stressed its significance for maintaining peace. In 1975, the relationship of human rights and international security was proclaimed by the Helsinki Final Act, which was signed by 35 countries including the U.S.S.R. and the United States. Among those rights are: the right to freedom of conscience; the right to receive and impart information within a country and across frontiers; the right to a free choice of one's country of residence and domicile within a country; freedom of religion; and freedom from psychiatric persecution. Finally, citizens have the right to control their national leaders' decision-making in matters on which the fate of the world depends. But we don't even know how, or by whom, the decision to invade Afghanistan was made! People in our country do not have even a fraction of the information about events in the world and in their own country which the citizens of the West have at their disposal. The opportunity to criticize the policy of one's national leaders in matters of war and peace as you do freely is, in our country, entirely absent. Not only critical statements but those merely factual in nature, made on even much less important questions, often entail arrest and a long sentence of confinement or psychiatric prison.

In keeping with the general nature of this letter, I refrain here from citing many specific examples, but must mention the fate of Anatoly Shcharansky, who is wasting away in Chistopol Prison for the right to be visited by his mother and to write to her,* and Yuri Orlov who, now for a third time, has been put for six months in the punishment block of a Perm labor camp, after having been beaten unmercifully in the presence of a warden.

In December 1982 there was an amnesty to honor the U.S.S.R.'s sixtieth anniversary but, just as in 1977 and in the preceding amnesties, there was a point made of excluding prisoners of conscience. So distant is the U.S.S.R. from the principles it proclaims, a country which bears such great responsibility for the fate of the world!

IX

In conclusion I again stress how important it is that the world realize the absolute inadmissibility of nu-

* *Editor's Note.* At the time this Open Letter was written Shcharansky was on a hunger strike, because he was denied all contact with his family. He has since been permitted an exchange of letters with his mother, and has ended his fast.

clear war, the collective suicide of mankind. It is impossible to win a nuclear war. What is necessary is to strive, systematically though carefully, for complete nuclear disarmament based on strategic parity in conventional weapons. As long as there are nuclear weapons in the world, there must be a strategic parity of nuclear forces so that neither side will venture to embark on a limited or regional nuclear war. Genuine security is possible only when based on a stabilization of international relations, a repudiation of expansionist policies, the strengthening of international trust, openness and pluralization in the socialist societies, the observance of human rights throughout the world, the rapprochement—convergence—of the socialist and capitalist systems, and worldwide coordinated efforts to solve global problems.

February 2, 1983   *Andrei Sakharov*

Andrei Sakharov is the distinguished Soviet physicist, winner of the 1975 Nobel Peace Prize, currently in internal exile in Gorki. Among his works available in English are *Alarm and Hope* and *Collected Scientific Works*. The translation from the Russian of this open letter to Sidney Drell was done by Richard Lourie and Efrem Yankelevich. Copyright © Andrei Sakharov.

Professor Sidney Drell is Lewis M. Terman Professor, Deputy Director, and Executive Head of Theoretical Physics at the Stanford Linear Accelerator Center, one of the world's leading accelerators of high energy particles. He is also a Faculty Fellow and founding member of Stanford University's Arms Control and Disarmament Program.

His scientific contributions have made him an international leader in theoretical high energy physics and have won him many professional honors, including election to the National Academy of Sciences and the American Academy of Arts and Sciences, and the award of the Ernest O. Lawrence Memorial Award for research in Theoretical Physics by the U.S. Atomic Energy Commission.

Professor Drell combines major professional accomplishments with broad intellectual and social interests. For more than twenty years he has served in various capacities as an adviser to the U.S. government on issues of national security and arms control. These activities have included membership on the President's Science Advisory Committee and consulting for the National Security Council and the Arms Control and Disarmament Agency. He currently advises executive agencies and the Congress on defense and intelligence issues. He serves on the Board of Directors of the Arms Control Association in Washington, D.C., and is active in the American Committee on East-West Accord in Washington, D.C. In 1980 Dr. Drell received the Leo Szilard Award for Physics in the Public Interest from the Forum on Physics and Society of the American Physical Society.

He received his Bachelor of Arts degree from Princeton University and his Master of Arts and Doctor of Philosophy degrees from the University of Illinois.